Physical Characteristic of the Dachshund

(from The American Kennel Club breed standard)

Croup: Long, rounded and full, sinking slightly toward the tail.

Trunk: Long and fully muscled. When viewed in profile, the back lies in the straightest possible line between the withers and the short very slightly arched loin. Abdomen slightly drawn up.

Hindquarters Strong and cleanly muscled. From the rear, the thighs are strong and powerful. The legs turn neither in nor out.

Tail: Set in continuation of the spine, extending without kinks, twists, or pronounced curvature, and not carried too gaily.

Size: Bred and shown in two sizes, standard and miniature. Miniatures: "11 pounds and under at 12 months of age and older." Standards: usually between 16 and 32 pounds.

Hind Paws: Smaller than the front paws with four compactly closed and arched toes with tough, thick pads.

Coat: The Dachshund is bred with three varieties of coat: (1) Smooth; (2) Wirehaired; (3) Longhaired.

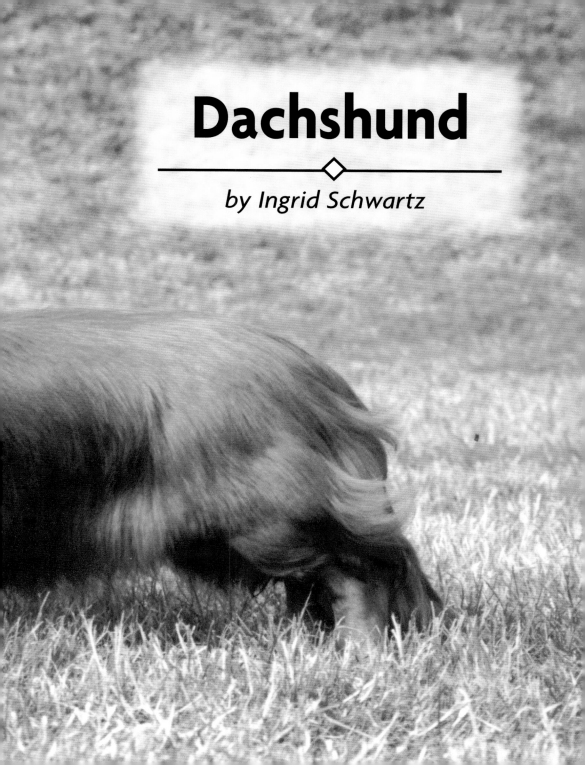

Dachshund

◇

by Ingrid Schwartz

Contents

Photographs by:
Norvia Behling, T. J. Calhoun, Carolina Biological Supply, Doskocil, Isabelle Français, James Hayden-Yoav, James R. Hayden, RBP, Bill Jonas, Carol Ann Johnson, Dwight R. Kuhn, Dr. Dennis Kunkel, Cary C. Manaton, John Merriman, Mikki Pet Products, Phototake, Jean Claude Revy, Alice Roche, Dr. Andrew Spielman, Bill Tacke, Alice van Kempen and C. James Webb.

The publisher wishes to thank Leigh Conant, Carolyn Galant, Helen Hamilton, Joanmarie Lermann, Pete Lewis, Phil Lewis, Terri McCready, John Merriman, John & Paula Murray, Pamela Richards, Patricia Riley, Veronica Smith, Bill Tacke and the rest of the owners of dogs featured in this book.

Illustrations by Renée Low

KENNEL CLUB BOOKS® DACHSHUND
ISBN: 1-59378-254-3

Copyright © 2003, **2007** • Kennel Club Books® • A Division of BowTie, Inc.
40 Main Street, Freehold, NJ 07728 USA
Cover Design Patented: US 6,435,559 B2 • Printed in South Korea

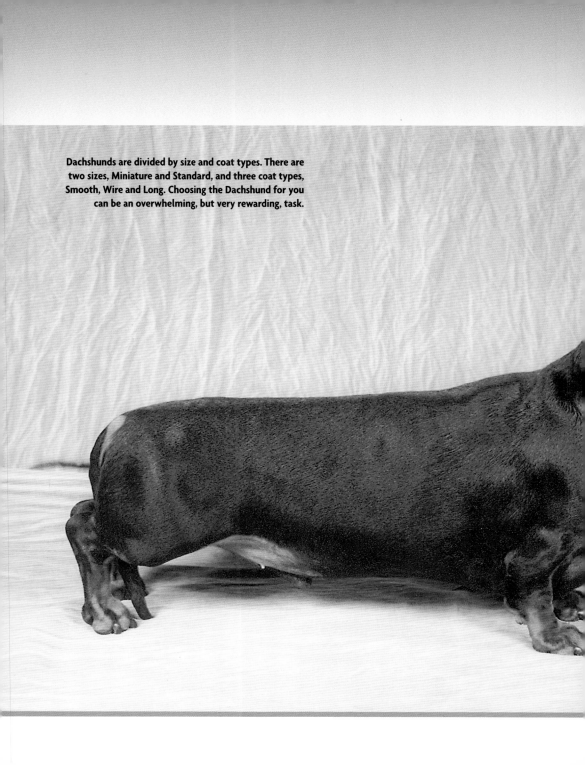

Dachshunds are divided by size and coat types. There are two sizes, Miniature and Standard, and three coat types, Smooth, Wire and Long. Choosing the Dachshund for you can be an overwhelming, but very rewarding, task.

HISTORY OF THE
DACHSHUND

Saying you would like to have a Dachshund is similar to going into a candy store and saying you would like to have some chocolate. There are many kinds of chocolates and many kinds of Dachshunds. You have to decide which kind you would like.

Dachshunds come in many varieties. There are different sizes and colors as well as types of coat to choose from, each with its own characteristics and group of devoted owners and admirers.

Basically, Dachshunds are long-bodied, short-legged dogs—small in stature but very large in personality—whose noses are so close to the ground that not much escapes their notice! In fact, their physical structure is the primary reason for their hunting expertise. This scenting ability was recognized by German hunters as early as the 15th century.

Derived from early German hounds known as *Deutsche Bracken*, these little dogs were called badger dogs or diggers. Eventually they were crossed with small terrier-type dogs to produce the Dachshunds we

Dachshund

FORM AND FUNCTION

Since dogs have been inbred for centuries, their physical and mental characteristics are constantly being changed to suit man's desires for hunting, retrieving, scenting, guarding and warming their masters' laps. During the past 150 years, dogs have been judged according to physical characteristics as well as functional abilities. Few breeds can boast a genuine balance between physique, working ability and temperament.

This is the first known illustration that shows both Wirehaired and Longhaired Dachshunds. It dates from 1876 and was rendered by E. C. Ash.

know today. With the nose of the hound, the long, low body that burrows into holes in the ground and the fearless terrier-like enthusiasm for the chase, the Dachshund is hard to beat.

Early artistic illustrations and sculptures from the 15th, 16th and 17th centuries show Dachshund-type dogs hunting badgers. A statue of an early Egyptian pharaoh also has a Dachshund-type dog named "Teckel" on it. In each depiction, the characteristics of strength, stamina, courage and keenness were clearly illustrated.

Dachshunds come in two sizes, Standard and Miniature. Originally, Standard Dachshunds weighed between 30 and 35 pounds and were used in packs to catch wild boar. The modern-day Dachshund, however, weighs in at considerably less, 16 to 32 pounds at most.

Miniatures originally weighed from 16 to 25 pounds and hunted fox or tracked wounded deer. Today, the average Miniature weighs from 8 to 12 pounds and hunts rabbit or hare. Occasionally, a Miniature of only 5 to 6 pounds will be used in hunting, providing that the dog possesses plenty of hunting spirit that serves to offset his diminutive size.

There are three varieties of

DEER TRACKER

The tracking of downed deer was the Miniature Dachshund's original purpose in Germany. The term *Vorstehhund* referred to an all-purpose hunting dog, usually a cross between a Bloodhound (*Schweisshund*) and a Pointer. The Miniature Dachshund was able to use its fine nose and its low-to-the-ground stature, making it an exceptional tracking dog.

The Dachshund and the terrier breeds are not so far removed. They share some common ancestors and their love of all things dirty, as these two sandy pals illustrate.

coat in Dachshunds: Smooth, Longhaired and Wirehaired. The Smooth and Longhaired varieties were developed first. The Wirehaired variety was developed later for hunting in briars and thorn bushes.

Coat colors offer something for every Dachshund lover. Red, cream, bi-color, black, chocolate, wild boar, gray-blue, fawn,

dappled and brindle are colors/color combinations that can be found wherever Dachshunds are bred. Regardless of size, coat type or color, all Dachshunds possess exceptional scenting and digging abilities, which make them ideal hunters.

DACHSHUNDS IN THE FATHERLAND

The breed began its formal organization when a standard of perfection for the breed was established in the *Deutscher Hunde-Stammbuch* (the "German Hound Family Tree Book"). It covered Smooth and

This old wood-engraved print, circa 1700, was captioned as *The Badger-Dog at Work*. The woodcut shows Dachshunds at various stages of badger hunting.

11

Longhaireds when the first volume of this stud book was produced in 1840. Half a century later, in 1890, Wirehaireds were included in the book. The book was published until 1935, when it was discontinued.

During the latter half of the 1800s, several hunting Dachshund associations kept their own stud books. These clubs recorded only those dogs that had proved their hunting ability; they were not concerned about the coats or conformation of the dogs listed. The dogs' accomplishments in the field were the sole criteria for inclusion in the hunting stud books.

Clubs devoted exclusively to the various Dachshund coat types also existed during this period, but no special identi-

The Countess Reventlow of Denmark, an outstanding judge circa 1930, judging Wirehaired Dachshunds. Note the dappled coloring of the dog farther from the camera.

fying initials were given to define the coat types of the dogs listed in the stud books. That changed, too, in 1915.

The following designations were created: The initial "K" stood for *Kurzhaar* (Smooth); "R" for *Rauhhaar* (Wirehaired); "L" for *Langhaar* (Longhaired); and "Z" for *Zwerg* (Miniature). Henceforth, the defining initial would be added to the registration number of all Dachshunds listed under the *Teckelklub* (German Dachshund Club).

Management of the breed initially was conducted by two

TECKEL, TECKEL, TECKEL

In Germany, Dachshunds are measured by the size of the hole that the dog can enter (in pursuit of game), as opposed to pounds or inches like most other breeds. The Germans divide the breed into three categories, not two. The Standard Dachshund is known as the *Normalgrossteckel,* and the Miniature Dachshund, divided into two categories, is called *Zwergteckel* (meaning dwarf) and *Kaninchenteckel* (meaning rabbit). These latter *teckels* measure 13.8 inches around the chest for the *Zwergteckel,* and 11.8 inches for the *Kaninchenteckel.*

German Scenthounds

The Dachshund is the only German hound that enjoys popularity outside its homeland. There are at least four

The Bavarian Mountain Hound.

other German scenthound breeds, including the Deutsche Bracke, one of the Dachshund's ancestors; the Westphalian Dachsbracke, another short-legged hound; the Hanoverian Hound and the Bavarian Mountain Hound.

DACHSHUNDS IN THE USA

In America, Dachshunds have not been used for hunting ground game such as badger and wild boar nor for tracking wounded deer. However, the dogs' sterling qualities of lively character, courage and devotion have always made them very popular. As a matter of fact, Dachshunds were imported into America well before the American Kennel Club initiated its stud book in 1885.

By 1895, the Dachshund Club of America advanced the breed's popularity by promoting the hunting aspects of the dogs through badger-dog hunting trials. In 1913, Dachshunds were listed among the ten most popular breeds in America. When World War I began, Dachshund interest declined and remained low until the early 1930s. By 1940, they were again ranked among the top ten breeds in America and maintained that standing into the 21st century.

One of the long-legged German scenthounds, the Deutsche Bracke is one of the Dachshund's early ancestors.

groups: the Teckelklub, founded in 1888, handled bench conformation shows, and the *Gebrauchsteckel Klub* conducted hunting activities. In 1935, the two groups combined their stud books and activities into the FD-RDG, the *Fachschaft Dachshunde im Reichsverband fur das Deutsche Hundewesen.* After World War II, the Deutscher once again resumed management of the breed.

While in Germany, Miniature Dachshunds are shown in a special class for dogs weighing less than nine pounds, this is not the case in the USA. In America, Standard and Miniature Dachshunds compete in the same class, with dogs weighing 11 pounds or under at 12 months of age being shown in a special division.

DACHSHUNDS IN THE UK
England established a Dachshund specialty club even before one was begun in Germany. Indeed, despite the problems created by World War I, England claimed six noted Dachshund breeders who adhered to a strict breeding code throughout the war. Though these breeders were often referred to as "pro-German" or "German sympathizers," they held firm to the integrity of the Dachshund in order to preserve its genetic foundation. Moreover, their efforts to protect the early gene pool succeeded.

Two of the earliest English Dachshunds to leave an indelible mark on the breed in the 1890s were Jackdaw, owned by Harry Jones of Ipswich, and Pterodactyl, owned by Sidney Woodiwiss. Those early ancestors still influence the breed today.

Australia, Denmark, Holland and India are also countries where Dachshunds are popular. In the UK, the Miniature Longhaired Dachshund is the favorite hound, even outnumbering such British hounds as the Basset, the Beagle and the Whippet, the latter being the second most popular.

A DOG BY ANY OTHER NAME

The term *Dachshund* is not without its equivalents: in France, the term is *basset*, and in Switzerland, the term is *neider*. Native low-legged breeds represent this terminology, such the Petit Basset

The Petit Basset Griffon Vendéen.

Griffon Vendéen and the Basset Fauve de Bretagne in France, and the Schweizer Neiderlaufhund and the Berner Neiderlaufhund in Switzerland.

The beauty and personality of the Dachshund have fascinated artists for generations. This famous painting of Earl Satin was created by Lilian Cheviot in 1906.

The Dachshund is, quite simply, the "right dog" for many people. Small in size, even the largest Standard Dachshund weighs only about 30 pounds. Easy to maintain in good physical condition, the Dachshund doesn't require long runs over many acres. Possessing a friendly, companionable personality, the Dachshund charms his way into the hearts of all who get to know him.

Though he can be rather stubborn at times, his behavior

easily can be modified by a wise owner who quickly changes the subject and gets the dog to focus on some new activity. In other words, the owner refuses to recognize the dog's obstinacy and thereby prevents a repetition of the undesirable behavior. Physical rough handling only makes an even-tempered Dachshund become aggressive.

The fact that Dachshunds love people, especially children and the elderly, endears them to the general population. Indeed, Dachshunds are among the most popular breeds of dog in the USA, Germany and Britain. Although the original purpose of hunting is no longer the main reason to breed Dachshunds, they possess

Dachshunds are dogs that appeal to many people because they are friendly, intelligent and portable.

so many other desirable qualities that they will retain their popular status for many years to come.

However, for the few Dachshund owners who are interested in preserving that hunting trait, there are Dachshund field trials. In America, trials were instituted in 1935. These competitions judge the dogs' ability and style in finding and retrieving game such as rabbits. The dogs must possess good noses (to smell the prey), courage to pursue the prey, keenness for the hunt, perseverance and willingness to get the job done.

All Dachshunds, regardless of variety or size, compete together in field trials. At a trial, a Dachshund is a Dachshund. There are, however, various stakes or classes for dogs of different ages and experience. Once a dog earns a field trial champion title, he enters the Dachshund history book of distinction and his progeny are much sought after.

The rules for field trials, obedience and agility competitions, and breed conformation classes, are spelled out in detail by both breed clubs and kennel clubs. In order to produce dogs that will achieve success in competition, whether conformation or performance events, breeders must understand the criteria set forth in their breed's standard as well as the abilities that the dogs must possess.

DOGS, DOGS, GOOD FOR YOUR HEART!

People usually purchase dogs for companionship, but studies show that dogs can help to improve their owners' health and level of activity, as well as lower a human's risk of coronary heart disease. Without even realizing it, when a person puts time into exercising, grooming and feeding a dog, he also puts more

time into his own personal health care. Dog owners establish more routine schedules for their dogs to follow, which can have positive effects on a human's health. Dogs also teach us patience, offer unconditional love and provide the joy of having a furry friend to pet!

Dachshunds are odorless and exceptionally clean dogs. The Miniature is mature by 12 months of age, while the Standard may not be fully mature until he reaches 18 months of age. Dachshunds are exceptionally long-lived dogs, with many living until 12 to 14 years of age. Regardless of size or variety, the Dachshund is easily maintained and managed, thus making it a most desirable companion.

ONE-PERSON DOG

Some Dachshunds will attempt to attach themselves to only one person in a

family while ignoring the other family members. This situation can be avoided if the entire family participates in activities with the dog as well as practices obedience exercises with him. The dog must learn that he is part of the whole family pack, not just one isolated member.

WHO MAKES AN IDEAL DACHSHUND OWNER?

The ideal Dachshund owner is a person who enjoys life with his dog and also enjoys the company of other people. Dachshunds are very social dogs, though they are often particularly devoted to one owner. The Dachshund is always interested in doing enjoyable things within its own physical capabilities. Therefore, the person who will derive the most pleasure from owning and living with a Dachshund is a gregarious individual who chooses activities that can include his dog.

Playing with the dog indoors and out, the owner finds fetch games of particular interest to Dachshunds. Participating in obedience and agility competitions is most rewarding for owner and dog alike. Visiting the park and taking reasonable walks are also much enjoyed by your little companion. Of course, snuggling beneath the covers on a cold, rainy day is always at the top of any Dachshund's list of favorite things to do. Thus, an individual who enjoys a lazy afternoon with a good book and a Dachshund also makes an ideal owner.

Finally, because of the Dachshund's intelligence and versatility, the ideal owner is a person who has time to spend and interests to share with his dog. Dachshunds do not like being left alone for long periods of time and then, once the owner comes home, being ignored even more of the time. Dachshunds do best when they're mentally stimulated and made to feel appreciated and like members of the family.

BREED VERSATILITY

I'd like you now to meet two Dachshunds I know. Both are very much loved by their families and both are happy dogs, yet they have very different lifestyles.

"Whiskers" is a one-year-old neutered male. He's a Longhaired Standard, black and tan in color. By nature he's a quiet dog who loves children and family friends. He's typically "Dachshund stubborn," yet easily trained because he enjoys learning new things and doing things with his owners. Whiskers gets on well with other dogs and particularly loves a four-year-old female mixed-breed who shares his home. He also does well with other household residents, such as the two cats and two hamsters. When asked what was the best thing about Whiskers, the owners responded quickly, "He's very mellow—like us!"

Now meet "Tootsie." She's a Smooth Miniature, red in color, who was deserted by her owners at three-and-a-half years of age. Fortunately for Tootsie, she was rescued by a lady who enjoyed dog obedience competition and had always wanted to own a

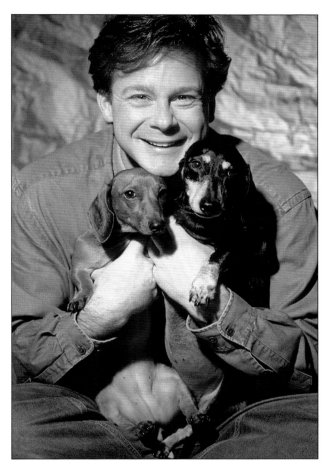

Dachshund. Tootsie began obedience training and soon amassed a list of obedience wins that would impress even the toughest judge, quickly earning her title. Then she began agility training and fell in love with the sport. Today, at ten years of age, Tootsie has earned four agility titles in two organizations. The list of Tootsie's accomplishments

The ideal Dachshund owner is devoted to the breed, always delighted to spend time bonding with and caring for his dogs. Owners, John Merriman and Bill Tacke.

The lovely Elsa is enjoying a sunny afternoon in the garden. Now in her senior years, Elsa still retains her Dachshund spirit and affectionate personality.

encounters. She does, however, love having guests visit their home and is an excellent ambassador for all Dachshunds. Her owner reports that, having lived with Tootsie for seven years, she would never be without a Dachshund. "They are even better than I thought they'd be!" she claims.

Despite the differences in lifestyle between Whiskers and Tootsie, both dogs are well-adjusted and cherished members of their human families. These two dogs serve as examples of how versatile the Dachshund can be as he makes his life with humans and brings his owners great pleasure and comfort.

is almost bigger than she is!

At home, Tootsie sleeps in owner Sunny Simpson's bed under the covers (a place familiar to many Dachshunds). Although Tootsie was never socialized with children when she was a young puppy, she tolerates them as long as her owner supervises the

Given the long back of the Dachshund and its short legs, the breed encounters certain problems of which owners must be keenly aware. This young Wire-haired Miniature Dachshund appears to be the picture of good health.

HEALTH CONCERNS IN DACHSHUNDS

Generally speaking, most dogs are square creatures, about as high from the ground to the top of their shoulders as they are from the front of their chests to their rumps. Each of their four legs is placed directly under the trunk of the body at the four corners. Their necks are gently arched and their heads balance out their body size: little heads for little dogs, big heads for big dogs. Dachshunds, however, are different. Their long, low-to-the-ground body type resembles a train with an engine in the front, a caboose at the end and the cars in the middle. Their long, swaying tails even add to their length, to accentuate how very different they are!

Because of their unique skeletal structure, Dachshunds have the potential to experience both environmental and genetic problems common to long-bodied dogs. Living in an environment that is oblivious to their special conformation, Dachshunds often are subjected to many hazards. Jumping, excessive stair-climbing and other high-impact activities usually result in serious diseases and conditions of the vertebrae. When genetically inferior dogs are bred, they often produce genetically inferior puppies. These puppies, in turn, grow up to develop serious skeletal conditions that are difficult

YOUNG FRIENDS

When teaching a Dachshund to accept and like children, be sure that the

children move slowly rather than with erratic, fast motions. Dachshunds see fast-moving things as prey and will go after them, even though these "things" might be children. Once the dogs become accustomed to children, they will accept the running and playing of their young human friends.

and/or impossible to correct. In addition, overweight puppies are always at risk. There are many health conditions seen in dogs of many breeds, including Dachshunds. Let's review some of the major ones here.

MAJOR PROBLEMS

Intervertebral disk disease affects more Dachshunds than all other dogs combined, so naturally it is atop this list of conditions that concern Dachshund owners. Due to the Dachshund's long-backed construction, owners are advised

SIT!

If a Dachshund refuses to sit with both haunches squarely beneath him and,

instead, sits on one side or the other, he may have a physical reason for doing so. Discuss this habit with your veterinarian to be certain that the dog isn't suffering from some structural problem.

to avoid activities that will strain their backs and spines. IVD, as the disease is known, is marked by herniated disks in the lower back. The disease primarily affects dogs with stunted legs. Affected dogs experience severe pain, usually in the lower back but sometimes in the neck as well. The disease can be treated medically and/or surgically, depending on the severity. Carts for dogs have been devised to assist Dachshunds with rear-quarter paralysis due to severe IVD.

Acanthosis nigricans, unfortunately, seems to be unique to the Dachshund. It is characterized by dark, thick skin in Dachshund's groin and armpits. While the genetic origin of the disease is unclear, it is certain that affected dogs are not to be bred. Vitamin E supplementation has been used to improve the condition, though no cure is known.

Hypothyroidism, commonly confused with obesity in Dachshunds, is simply the insufficient production of thyroid hormones. In Dachshunds, lymphocytic thyroiditis is most common. Dogs are affected between ages one to three years. Less than half of the Dachshunds affected manifest obesity; most individuals experience recurrent infections and lack of energy. Diagnosis of hypothyroidism is often tricky, though the treatment tends to be direct and affordable.

Epilepsy is a seizure disorder that affects Dachshunds as well as many other breeds of dog. Epileptic dogs can be managed with various veterinary drugs, though some side effects exist, including temporary weakness and increased appetite and thirst.

EYE PROBLEMS

A cataract is a cloudiness or film over the lens of the eye, categorized by age of onset, location on the eye and stage of the cloudiness. As it is a hereditary condition, parents should be tested before breeding takes place to ensure that parents are not

BONE PROBLEMS

Surgery is often used to correct genetic bone diseases in dogs. Usually the problems present themselves early in the dog's life and must be treated before bone growth stops.

carrying the genes for cataracts.

Glaucoma, a leading cause of blindness in dogs, is caused by an increase in fluid pressure within the eye. This disease can be hereditary, so parents should be tested prior to breeding. Treatment for glaucoma can be medical or surgical, or both.

Progressive retinal atrophy (PRA), a series of inherited disorders affecting the retina of the eyes, causes visual impairment that is slow but progressive. Night blindness can be the first sign of trouble. There is no known way to stop onset.

Other eye conditions have also been known to occur in Dachshunds. This list is by no means complete, but is included here to make new owners aware of possible problems in the breed: corneal dystrophy, congenital night blindness, entropion, tear duct anomalies, wall eye, kerato-conjunctivitis, microphthalmia and ectasia syndrome.

ADDITIONAL PROBLEMS SEEN IN DACHSHUNDS

Discuss the following conditions with your veterinarian and/or your breeder. A better understanding of each of these

According to the AKC standard, the Longhaired's coat should be "sleek, glistening, often slightly wavy" and should give the dog an "elegant appearance."

problems will enlighten the new owner, making him more aware of the breed's congenital, hereditary and environmentally triggered problems. These potential problems include excessive hardening of the long bones, osteoporosis, cutaneous asthenia (also known as Ehlers-Danlos syndrome), renal hypoplasia (problem of the kidneys), diabetes, urinary tract problems and achondroplasia (a genetic bone disease). Hair changes, sluggishness and secondary infections are common and must be treated aggressively by a veterinarian. These symptoms are linked to a potential problem. Owners should be aware that deafness in dappled dogs and von Willebrand's disease (a common blood disease) are genetic.

It's important to note here that not all Dachshunds will suffer serious physical diseases or problems. However, it is important for the puppy buyer to be aware of the health conditions that can affect the dog he is about to purchase. Healthy parents and a well-informed, caring breeder are the best factors in producing healthy puppies. Many health problems in dogs today can be tested for in very young puppies. Reputable breeders usually have these tests performed so that they can send their puppies off to new homes with certificates of good health. Thus, the new owners can begin raising their puppy in the knowledge that they have chosen a healthy puppy from a quality source. In short, it all boils down to the old saying that knowledge is power—with humans *and* with dogs.

Dachshunds were bred for hunting badgers, thus they are constantly sniffing and staying in close contact with the earth.

MEDICAL PROBLEMS FREQUENTLY SEEN IN DACHSHUNDS

Condition	Age Affected	Cause	Area Affected
Acanthosis Nigricans	Adults	Unknown	Skin
Cataracts	Less than 1 Year	Congenital	Eyes
Cushing's Syndrome	Middle Age to Older	Pituitary Tumor	Endocrine System
Cystine Urolithiasis	Adults	Congenital	Urinary Tract
Elbow Dysplasia	4 to 7 Months	Congenital	Elbow Joint
Epilepsy	6 Months to 3 Years	Congenital	Nervous System
Hip Dysplasia	4 to 9 Months	Congenital	Hip Joint
Hypothyroidism	1 to 3 Years	Lymphocytic Thyroiditis	Endocrine System
Intervertebral Disk Disease	By 1 Year	Congenital	Spinal Column
Medial Patellar Luxation	Adults	Congenital	Kneecaps
Narcolepsy	1 to 5 Months	Congenital	Sleep Disorder
Sebaceous Adenitis	Young Adults	Congenital	Hair Follicles
Progressive Retinal Atrophy	6 to 12 Months	Congenital	Retina
Von Willebrand's Disease	Birth	Congenital	Blood

The standard of perfection for Dachshunds is a 'word picture' that describes what a Dachshund should look and act like. All dogs are judged against that imaginary image each time they enter the show ring. Although different standards for the Dachshund exist in different countries, each standard basically describes the very same dog. In all cases, the standard of perfection determines what is and what is not acceptable in the physical conformation and behavioral traits of the breed in question. In some countries, such as the USA, these standards are written by a national breed club and adopted and enforced by the country's kennel club. In other countries, such as England, the national kennel club both creates and enforces standards for each recognized breed for competition and championship status in the stud book.

In the first paragraph of the AKC standard, it rather boldly states that the dog should appear "neither crippled, awkward, nor cramped in his capacity for movement." The Dachshund's conformation should in no way interfere with its ability to move, including long-distance tracking and hunting.

The standard also includes the phrase "courageous to the point of rashness," which well defines this determined earthdog. The standard goes on to say, "Inasmuch as the Dachshund is a hunting dog, scars from honorable wounds shall not be considered a fault." This inclusion certainly shows how seriously breeders still consider the hunting spirit of the breed.

The standard of perfection goes into great detail to define each part of the body of the Dachshund. In addition, size, coat color and coat variety are described as the reader creates a mental picture of the ideal Dachshund. The AKC standard is

The breed standard for all six Dachshunds is identical, except the coat descriptions and size. This Standard Wirehaired has had a successful day in the ring.

very specific, using terms that may be unfamiliar to a fancier without breeding or judging experience. The following standard has been abridged to suffice as a guide for the pet owner. Those interested in showing are advised to research the full standard in detail.

THE AMERICAN KENNEL CLUB STANDARD FOR THE DACHSHUND

General Appearance: Low to ground, long in body and short of leg with robust muscular development, the skin is elastic and pliable without excessive wrinkling. Appearing neither crippled, awkward, nor cramped in his capacity for movement, the Dachshund is well-balanced with bold and confident head carriage and intelligent, alert facial expression. His hunting spirit, good nose, loud tongue and distinctive build make him well-suited for below-ground work and for beating the bush. His keen nose gives him an advantage over most other breeds for trailing. Note: Inasmuch as the Dachshund is a hunting dog, scars from honorable wounds shall not be considered a fault.

Size, Proportion, Substance: Bred and shown in two sizes, standard and miniature, miniatures are not a separate classification but compete in a class division for "11 pounds and under at 12 months of age and

---

BREEDER'S BLUEPRINT

If you are considering breeding your bitch, it is very important that you are familiar with the breed standard. Reputable breeders breed with the intention of producing dogs that are as

close as possible to the standard and that contribute to the advancement of the breed. Study the standard for both physical appearance and temperament, and make certain your bitch and your chosen stud dog measure up.

---

older." Weight of the standard size is usually between 16 and 32 pounds.

Head: Viewed from above or from the side, the head tapers uniformly to the tip of the nose. The eyes are of medium size, almond-shaped and dark-rimmed, with an energetic, pleasant expression; not piercing; very dark in color. Wall eyes, except in the case of dappled dogs, are a

Dachshund

Smooth Dachshund.

Wirehaired Dachshund.

Longhaired Dachshund.

serious fault. The ears are set near the top of the head, not too far forward, of moderate length, rounded, not narrow, pointed, or folded. Their carriage, when animated, is with the forward edge just touching the cheek so that the ears frame the face. The skull is slightly arched, neither too broad nor too narrow, and slopes gradually with little perceptible stop into the finely-formed, slightly arched muzzle. Black is the preferred color of the nose. Lips are tightly stretched, well covering the lower jaw. Nostrils well open. Jaws opening wide and hinged well back of the eyes, with strongly developed bones and teeth. *Teeth*—Powerful canine teeth; teeth fit closely together in a scissors bite. An even bite is a minor fault. Any other deviation is a serious fault.

Neck: Long, muscular, clean-cut, without dewlap, slightly arched in the nape, flowing gracefully into the shoulders.

Trunk: The trunk is long and fully muscled. When viewed in profile, the back lies in the straightest possible line between the withers and the short very slightly arched loin.

Forequarters: For effective underground work, the front must be strong, deep, long and cleanly muscled. Forequarters in detail: *Chest*—The breastbone is strongly prominent in front so that on either side a depression or dimple appears. The enclosing structure of well-sprung ribs appears full and oval to allow, by its ample capacity, complete development of heart and lungs. Viewed in profile, the lowest point of the breast line is covered by the front leg. *Shoulder Blades*— Long, broad, well-laid back... closely fitted at the withers, furnished with hard yet pliable muscles. *Upper Arm*—Ideally the same length as the shoulder blade and at right angles to the latter, strong of bone and hard of muscle, lying close to the ribs, with elbows close to the body, yet capable of free movement. *Forearm*—Short; supplied with hard yet pliable muscles on the front and outside. The joints between the forearms and the feet (wrists) are closer together than the shoulder joints, so that the front does not appear absolutely straight. Knuckling over is a disqualifying fault. *Feet*—Front paws are full, tight, compact, with well-arched toes and tough, thick pads. They may be equally inclined a trifle outward. There are five toes, four in use, close together with a pronounced arch and strong, short nails. Front dewclaws may be removed.

Hindquarters: Strong and cleanly muscled. From the rear, the thighs are strong and powerful. The legs turn neither in nor out. *Metatarsus*—Short and strong. When

MEETING THE IDEAL

The American Kennel Club defines a standard as: "A description of the ideal dog of each recognized breed, to serve as an ideal against which dogs are judged at shows." This "blueprint" is drawn up by

the breed's recognized parent club, approved by a majority of its membership and then submitted to the AKC for approval. The AKC states that "An understanding of any breed must begin with its standard. This applies to all dogs, not just those intended for showing."

viewed from behind, they are upright and parallel. *Feet—Hind Paws*—Smaller than the front paws with four compactly closed and arched toes with tough, thick pads.

Dachshund

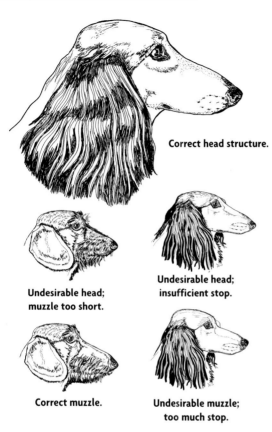

Correct head structure.

Undesirable head;
muzzle too short.

Undesirable head;
insufficient stop.

Correct muzzle.

Undesirable muzzle;
too much stop.

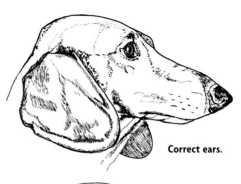

Correct ears.

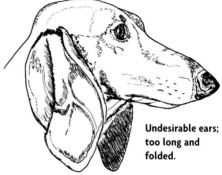

Undesirable ears;
too long and
folded.

The entire foot points straight ahead and is balanced equally on the ball and not merely on the toes. Rear dewclaws should be removed. *Croup*—Long, rounded and full, sinking slightly toward the tail. *Tail*—Set in continuation of the spine, extending without kinks, twists, or pronounced curvature, and not carried too gaily.

Gait: Fluid and smooth. Forelegs reach well forward, without much lift, in unison with the driving action of hind legs. The correct shoulder assembly and well-fitted elbows allow the long, free stride in front. Viewed in profile, the forward reach of the hind leg equals the rear extension. The thrust of correct movement is seen when the rear pads are clearly exposed during rear extension. Feet must travel parallel to the line of motion with no tendency to swing out, cross over, or interfere with each other. Short, choppy movement, rolling or high-stepping gait, close or overly wide coming or going are incorrect. The Dachshund must have agility, freedom of movement, and

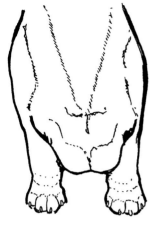

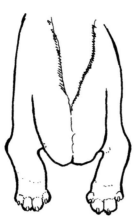

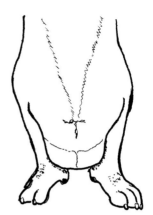

Correct forequarters.

Undesirable forequarters; elbows turning out.

Undesirable forequarters; toes out; weak feet.

endurance to do the work for which he was developed.

Temperament: The Dachshund is clever, lively and courageous to the point of rashness, persevering in above and below ground work, with all the senses well-developed. Any display of shyness is a serious fault.

Special Characteristics of the Three Coat Varieties: The Dachshund is bred with three varieties of coat: (1) Smooth; (2) Wirehaired; (3) Longhaired, and is shown in two sizes, standard and miniature. All

three varieties and both sizes must conform to the characteristics already specified. The following features are applicable for each variety:

Smooth Dachshund: *Coat—* Short, smooth and shining. Should be neither too long nor too thick. Ears not leathery. *Tail—*Gradually tapered to a point, well but not too richly haired. Long sleek bristles on the underside are considered a patch of strong-growing hair, not a fault. A brush tail is a fault, as is also a partly or wholly hairless tail. *Color of Hair*—Although base color

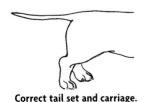

Correct tail set and carriage.

Acceptable tail carriage in repose.

Correct tail in the Longhaired, forming a "veritable flag."

Correct tail for Wirehaired Dachshund.

Incorrect tail; too long.

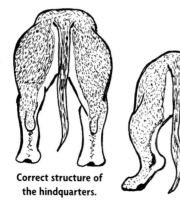

**Correct structure of
the hindquarters.**

Undesirable rear; cowhocks.

is immaterial, certain patterns and basic colors predominate. One-colored Dachshunds include red (with or without a shading of interspersed dark hairs or sable) and cream. A small amount of white on the chest is acceptable, but not desirable. *Nose and nails*—black.

Two-colored Dachshunds include black, chocolate, wild boar, gray (blue) and fawn (Isabella), each with tan markings over the eyes, on the sides of the jaw and underlip, on the inner edge of the ear, front, breast, inside and behind the front legs, on the paws and around the anus, and from there to about one-third to one-half of the length of the tail on the underside. Undue prominence or extreme lightness of tan markings is undesirable. A small amount of white on the chest is acceptable but not desirable. *Nose and nails*—in the case of black dogs, black; for chocolate and all other colors, dark brown, but self-colored is acceptable.

Dappled Dachshunds—The "single" dapple pattern is expressed as lighter-colored areas contrasting with the darker base color, which may be any acceptable color. Neither the light nor the dark color should predominate. Nose and nails are the same as for one and two-colored Dachshunds. Partial or wholly blue (wall) eyes are as acceptable as dark eyes. A large area of white on the chest of a dapple is permissible.

A "double" dapple is one in

Undesirable body; high in rear and low in front.

Correct body structure.

which varying amounts of white coloring occur over the body in addition to the dapple pattern. *Nose and nails:* as for one and two-color Dachshunds; partial or wholly self-colored is permissible.

Brindle is a pattern (as opposed to a color) in which black or dark stripes occur over the entire body although in some specimens the pattern may be visible only in the tan points.

Wirehaired Dachshund: *Coat*—With the exception of jaw, eyebrows, and ears, the whole body is covered with a uniform tight, short, thick, rough, hard, outer coat but with finer, somewhat softer, shorter hairs (undercoat) everywhere distributed between the coarser hairs. The absence of an undercoat is a fault. The distinctive facial furnishings include a beard and eyebrows. On the ears the hair is shorter than on the body, almost smooth. The general arrangement of

the hair is such that the wirehaired Dachshund, when viewed from a distance, resembles the smooth. Any sort of soft hair in the outercoat, wherever found on the body, especially on the top of the head, is a fault. The same is true of long, curly, or wavy hair, or hair that sticks out irregularly in all directions. *Tail*— Robust, thickly haired, gradually tapering to a point. A flag tail is a fault. *Color of Hair*—While the most common colors are wild boar, black and tan, and various shades of red, all colors are admissible. A small amount of white on the chest, although

Profile of underweight body.

Profile of body at ideal weight.

Profile of overweight body.

acceptable, is not desirable. *Nose and nails*—same as for the smooth variety.

Longhaired Dachshund: *Coat*—The sleek, glistening, often slightly wavy hair is longer under the neck and on the forechest, the underside of the body, the ears, and behind the legs. The coat gives the dog an elegant appearance. Short hair on the ear is not desirable. Too profuse a coat which masks type, equally long hair over the whole body, a curly coat, or a pronounced parting on the back are faults. *Tail*—Carried gracefully in prolongation of the spine; the hair attains its greatest length here and forms a veritable flag. *Color of Hair*—Same as for the smooth Dachshund. *Nose and nails*—same as for the smooth.

The foregoing description is that of the ideal Dachshund. Any deviation from the above described dog must be penalized to the extent of the deviation keeping in mind the importance of the contribution of the various features toward the basic original purpose of the breed.

Disqualification: Knuckling over of front legs.

Wirehaired Miniature Dachshunds, showing off their black and tan coats.

This Smooth Dachshund is being weighed before entering the Miniature division at a dog show. In the US, Dachshunds are divided by weight; in Germany, the breed's homeland, the breed is measured by the circumference of the dog's chest.

DACHSHUND

HOW TO SELECT A PUPPY

If you are convinced that the Dachshund is the ideal dog for you, it's time to learn about where to find a puppy and what to look for. Locating a litter of Dachshunds should not present a problem for the new owner. You should inquire about breeders in your area who enjoy a good reputation in the breed. You are looking for an established breeder with outstanding dog ethics and a strong commitment to the breed. New owners have as many questions as they have doubts. An established breeder is indeed the one to answer your many questions and make you comfortable with your choice of the Dachshund. An established breeder will sell you a puppy at a fair price if, and only if, the breeder determines that you are a suitable, worthy owner of his dogs. An established breeder can be relied upon for advice, no matter what time of day or night. A reputable breeder will accept a puppy back, without questions, should you decide that this is not the right dog for you.

When choosing a breeder, reputation is much more important than convenience of location. You are well advised to avoid the novice who lives only a few miles away. The local novice breeder, trying so

YOUR SCHEDULE . . .

If you lead an erratic, unpredictable life, with daily or weekly changes in your work requirements, consider the problems of owning a puppy. The new puppy has to be fed regularly, social-ized (loved, petted, handled, introduced to other people) and, most importantly, allowed to go outdoors for house-training. As the dog gets older, he can be more tolerant of deviations in his feeding schedule and times for relieving himself.

hard to find homes for his first litter of puppies, is more than accommodating and anxious to sell you one. Such a breeder will charge you as much as any established breeder. The novice breeder isn't going to interrogate you and your family about your intentions with the puppy, the environment and training you can provide, etc. However, you also will not be able to locate this elusive person should you suddenly need assistance with your poorly adjusted Dachshund puppy.

Choosing a breeder is an important first step in dog ownership. Fortunately, the majority of Dachshund breeders is devoted to the breed and its well-being. New owners should have little problem finding a reputable breeder who doesn't live in another state or on the other side of the country. The American Kennel Club is able to refer you to breeders of quality Dachshunds, as can any all-breed club or Dachshund club. Potential owners are encouraged to attend dog shows (or trials) to see the Dachshunds in action, to meet the owners and handlers firsthand and to get an idea of what Dachshunds look like outside a photographer's lens. Provided you approach the handlers when they are not terribly busy with the dogs, most are more than willing to

ARE YOU PREPARED?

Unfortunately, when a puppy is bought by someone who does not take into consideration the time and attention that dog ownership requires, it is the puppy who suffers when he is either abandoned or placed in a shelter by a frustrated owner. So all of the "homework" you do in preparation for

your pup's arrival will benefit you both. The more informed you are, the more you will know what to expect and the better equipped you will be to handle the ups and downs of raising a puppy. Hopefully, everyone in the household is willing to take responsibility and do his part in raising and caring for the pup. The anticipation of owning a dog often brings a lot of promises from excited family members: "I will walk him every day," "I will feed him," "I will house-train him," etc., but these things take time and effort, and promises can easily be forgotten once the novelty of the new pet has worn off.

wait as long as two years for a puppy. If you are really committed to the breeder whom you've selected, then you will wait (and hope for an early arrival!). If not, you may have to resort to your second- or third-choice breeder. Don't be too anxious, however. If the breeder doesn't have anyone interested in his puppies, there is probably a good reason.

Since breeding the

TEMPERAMENT COUNTS

Your selection of a good puppy can be determined by your needs. A show potential or a good pet? It is your choice. Every puppy, however, should be of good temperament. Although show-quality puppies are bred and raised with

emphasis on physical conformation, responsible breeders strive for equally good temperament. Do not buy from a breeder who concentrates solely on physical beauty at the expense of personality.

Meeting the pup is exciting and a bit overwhelming for the pup. Sometimes a timid pup will warm up to you after a 30-minute "let's-get-acquainted" session.

answer questions, recommend breeders and give advice.

Once you have contacted and met a breeder or two and made your choice about which breeder is best suited to your needs, it's time to visit the litter. Keep in mind that many top breeders have waiting lists. Sometimes new owners have to

Dachshund is a very delicate matter, and breeders must always test their breeding stock before producing a litter, most breeders are not expecting a litter every season, or, for that matter, even every year. Patience is a true Dachshund virtue.

Since you are likely to be choosing a Dachshund as a pet

PUPPY PERSONALITY

When a litter becomes available to you, choosing a pup out of all those adorable faces will not be an easy task! Sound temperament is of utmost importance, but each pup has its own personality and some may be better suited to you than others. A feisty, independent pup

will do well in a home with older children and adults, while quiet, shy puppies will thrive in a home with minimal noise and distractions. Your breeder knows the pups best and should be able to guide you in the right direction.

dog and not as a show or hunting dog, you simply should select a pup that is friendly and attractive. Dachshunds generally have relatively small litters, averaging five puppies, so selection is limited once you have located a desirable litter. Beware of the shy or overly aggressive puppy; be especially conscious of the nervous

Your puppy should have a well-fed appearance but not a distended abdomen, which may indicate worms or incorrect feeding, or both.

39

"YOU BETTER SHOP AROUND!"

Finding a reputable breeder who sells healthy pups is very important, but make sure that the breeder you choose is not only someone you respect but also someone with whom you feel comfortable. Your breeder will be a resource long after you buy your puppy, and you must be able to call with reasonable questions without being made to feel like a pest! If you don't connect on a personal level, investigate some other breeders before making a final decision.

Dachshund pup. Don't let sentiment or emotion trap you into buying the runt of the litter.

Try to divorce yourself from preconceived color preferences. Once you've found a healthy, socialized litter from a responsible, reputable breeder, in the coat variety of your choice, you do not want to struggle with color disappointment. Finding a dappled Longhaired puppy or a chocolate and fawn Wirehaired puppy will be far more difficult than simply locating a quality Long or Wire puppy. All the Dachshund colors and color combinations are attractive, so keep health and sound breeding foremost in your selection and worry about color last.

Breeders commonly allow visitors to see the litter by around the fifth or sixth week, and puppies leave for their new homes between the eighth and tenth week. Breeders who permit their puppies to leave earlier are more interested in your money than in their puppies' well-being. Puppies need to learn the rules of the trade from their dams, and most dams continue teaching the pups manners and dos and don'ts until around the eighth week. Breeders spend significant amounts of time with the Dachshund toddlers so that they are able to interact with the "other species," i.e., humans. Given the long history that dogs and humans have, bonding between the two species is natural but must be nurtured. A well-bred, well-socialized Dachshund pup wants nothing more than to be near you and to please you.

Finally, does the breeder have proper registration papers to go with the puppy of your choice? The breeder should also provide you with a feeding schedule and whatever else you will need to make the puppy's transition from its birth home to your home as easy and as stress-free as possible.

A pedigree is also an important document to get with your puppy. A pedigree is the history of your puppy's family tree. It tells you the registered

INHERIT THE MIND

In order to know whether or not a puppy will fit into your lifestyle, you need to assess his personality. A good way to do this is to interact with his parents. Your pup inherits not only his appearance but also his personality and temperament from the sire and dam. If the parents are fearful or overly aggressive, these same traits may show up in your puppy.

names of the parents, grandparents and great-grandparents on both the puppy's mother's and father's side. It also lists any degrees and/or titles that those relatives might have earned. The information that a pedigree provides can help you understand more about the physical conformation and/or behavioral accomplishments of your puppy's family. Remember that no amount of love and caring can compensate for genetic mistakes.

A simple example of inferior quality in dogs is a puppy with congenital dental

Astrid has just arrived at her new home. This lovely chocolate Miniature female is the new acquisition of Dachshund enthusiasts Bill Tacke and John Merriman.

How Vaccines Work

If you've just bought a puppy, you surely know the importance of having your pup vaccinated, but do you understand how vaccines work? Vaccines contain

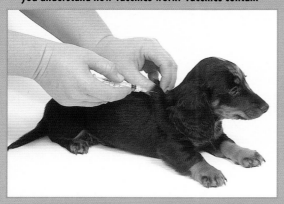

the same bacteria or viruses that cause the disease you want to prevent, but they have been chemically modified so that they don't cause any harm. Instead, the vaccine causes your dog to produce antibodies that fight the harmful bacteria. Thus, if your pup is exposed to the disease in the future, the antibodies will destroy the viruses or bacteria.

purchase a puppy from quality parents so that you and your new canine friend will enjoy a happy, healthy life together.

When studying the pedigree of a dog, look for indications that the dog's ancestors were active, successful achievers in various areas of the dog sport. For example, obedience titles are indicated by letters after the dogs' names. Obedience competition defines a dog's willingness to work with and obey its master in various behaviors such as heeling (walking beside the owner without pulling on the lead), staying when the owner leaves him for short periods and coming when he's called, despite environmental distractions.

Letters that precede a dog's name indicate championship status, denoting excellence in conformation events or perhaps the ultimate titles in field, obedience or agility trials.

Hunting and working titles tell us about the dogs' achievements in the field. Studying a pedigree that shows several ancestors with working titles indicates that the individual whose pedigree we're considering has a good chance of carrying some of those desirable genes. Usually the quality of the pedigree dictates the price of the puppy, so

problems, which are sometimes found in Dachshunds. When the mouth and teeth are malformed, the dog cannot eat and chew food properly. This, in turn, causes swallowing, digestive and elimination problems. Thus, the dog suffers all his life with stomach and elimination pain. Even his growth can be affected by dental problems. That's why it is so important to

expect to pay a higher price for a higher quality puppy. However, chances are that you will be rewarded by the quality of life that you and your pedigreed puppy will enjoy!

COMMITMENT OF OWNERSHIP

After considering all of these factors, you have most likely already made some very important decisions about selecting your puppy. You have chosen a Dachshund, which means that you have decided which characteristics you want in a dog and what type of dog will best fit into your family and lifestyle. If you have selected a breeder, you have gone a step further—you have done your research and found a responsible, conscientious person who breeds quality Dachshunds and who should be a reliable source of help as you and your puppy adjust to life together. If you have observed a litter in action, you have obtained a firsthand look at the dynamics of a puppy "pack" and, thus, you should have learned about each pup's individual personality—perhaps you have even found one that particularly appeals to you.

However, even if you have not yet found the Dachshund puppy of your dreams, observing pups will help you

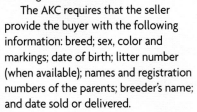

PEDIGREE VS. REGISTRATION

Too often new owners are confused between these two important documents. Your puppy's pedigree, essentially a family tree, is a written record of a dog's genealogy of three generations or more. The pedigree will show you the names as well as performance titles of all the dogs in your pup's background. Your breeder must provide you with a registration application, with his part properly filled out. You must complete the application and send it to the AKC with the proper fee. Every puppy must come from a litter that has been AKC-registered by the breeder, born in the USA and from a sire and dam that are also registered with the AKC.

The AKC requires that the seller provide the buyer with the following information: breed; sex, color and markings; date of birth; litter number (when available); names and registration numbers of the parents; breeder's name; and date sold or delivered.

learn to recognize certain behaviors and to determine what a pup's behavior indicates about his temperament. You will be able to pick out which pups are the leaders, which ones are less outgoing, which ones are confident, which ones are shy, playful, friendly, aggressive, etc. Equally as important, you will learn to recognize what a healthy pup should look and act like. All of these things will help you in your search, and when you find the Dachshund that was meant for you, you will know it!

Researching your breed, selecting a responsible breeder and observing as many pups as possible are all important steps on the way to dog ownership. It may seem like a lot of effort... and you have not even brought the pup home yet! Remember, though, you cannot be too careful when it comes to deciding on the type of dog you want and finding out about your prospective pup's background. Buying a puppy is not—or

WHAT'S AN ILP?

Pure-bred dogs without AKC registrations still have the opportunity to participate in non-conformation competition such as obedience, agility, tracking, earthdog trials and the like, provided the dog is pure-bred and of a breed registerable with the AKC. An ILP (Indefinite Listing Privilege) number is provided by the AKC and, although not a substitute for a registration number, allows dogs to compete in performance events. ILP dogs cannot be used for breeding; therefore, proof that the dog has been spayed/neutered is among the information that must accompany the ILP application.

Not to worry—in no time your Dachshund will feel comfortable and will want to be close to you every hour of the day.

should not be—just another whimsical purchase. This is one instance in which you actually do get to choose your own family! You may be thinking that buying a puppy should be fun—it should not be so serious and so much work. Keep in mind that your puppy is not a cuddly stuffed toy or decorative lawn ornament, but a creature that will become a real member of your family. You will come to realize that, while buying a puppy is a pleasurable and exciting endeavor, it is not something to be taken lightly. Relax...the fun will start when the pup comes home!

Always keep in mind that a puppy is nothing more than a baby in a furry disguise...a baby who is virtually helpless in a human world and who trusts his owner for fulfillment of his basic needs for survival. In addition to food, water and shelter, your pup needs care, protection, guidance and love. If you are not prepared to commit to this, then you are not prepared to own a dog.

Wait a minute, you say. How hard could this be? All of my neighbors own dogs and they seem to be doing just fine. Why should I have to worry about all of this? Well, you should not worry about it; in fact, you will probably find that once your Dachshund pup gets used to his new home, he will fall into his place in the family quite naturally. But it never hurts to emphasize the commitment of dog ownership. With some time and patience, it is really not too difficult to raise a curious and exuberant Dachshund pup to be a well-adjusted and well-mannered adult dog—a dog that could be your most loyal friend.

BOY OR GIRL?

An important consideration to be discussed is the sex of your puppy. For a family companion, a bitch may be the better choice, considering the female's inbred concern for all young creatures and her accompanying tolerance and patience. It is always advisable to spay a pet bitch, which may guarantee her a longer life.

QUALITY FOOD

The cost of food must be mentioned. All dogs need a good-quality food with an adequate supply of protein to develop their bones and muscles properly. Most dogs are not picky eaters but, unless fed properly on a balanced and nutritionally complete diet, can quickly succumb to skin problems.

Getting acquainted with your new charge will be priority number-one. Try not to overwhelm the puppy in his first days in your home. Let him settle in at his own pace.

PREPARING PUPPY'S PLACE IN YOUR HOME

Researching your breed and finding a breeder are only two aspects of the "homework" you will have to do before taking your Dachshund puppy home. You will also have to prepare your home and family for the new addition. Much as you would prepare a nursery for a newborn baby, you will need to designate a place in your home that will be the puppy's own. How you prepare your home will depend on how much freedom the dog will be allowed. In the case of the Dachshund, designating a couple of rooms (without stairs) for the puppy is ideal. Puppies should not be permitted to jump up on furniture nor to maneuver on stairs, both activities that can injure the puppy's long back. These activities should be forbidden from the very beginning so that your puppy understands that he belongs "low to the ground," as he was created!

When you bring your new puppy into your home, you are bringing him into what will become his home as well. Obviously, you did not buy a puppy so that he could "rule the roost," but in order for a puppy to grow into a stable, well-adjusted dog, he has to feel comfortable in his surroundings. Remember, he is leaving the warmth and security of his mother and littermates, as well as the familiarity of the only place he has ever known, so it is important to make his transition as easy as possible. By preparing a place in your home for the puppy, you are making him feel as welcome as possible in a strange new place. It should not take him long to get used to it, but the sudden shock of being transplanted is somewhat traumatic for a young pup. Imagine how a small child would feel in the same situation—that is how your puppy must be feeling. It

TIME TO GO HOME

Breeders rarely release puppies until they are eight to ten weeks of age. This is an acceptable age for most breeds of dog, excepting toy breeds, which are not released until around 12 weeks, given their petite sizes. If a breeder has a puppy that is 12 weeks of age or older, it is likely well socialized and housebroken. Be sure that it is otherwise healthy before deciding to bring it home.

is up to you to reassure him and to let him know, "Little *teckel*, you are going to like it here!"

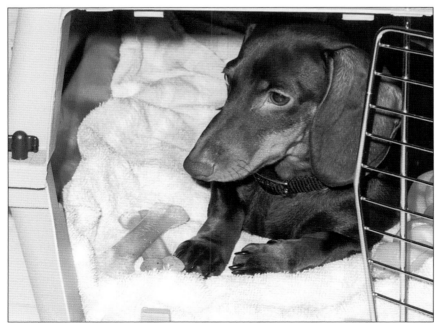

Provide a cozy crate for your Dachshund, with a soft blanket and some favorite toys.

PHOTO COURTESY OF DOSKOCIL.

Pet shops sell well-made, safe crates for dogs.

WHAT YOU SHOULD BUY

CRATE

To someone unfamiliar with the use of crates in dog training, it may seem like punishment to shut a dog in a crate, but this is not the case at all. Although all breeders do not advocate crate training, more and more breeders and trainers are recommending crates as a preferred tool for show puppies as well as pet puppies. Crates are not cruel—crates have many humane and highly effective uses in dog care and training. For example, crate training is a very popular and very successful housebreaking method. A crate can keep your dog safe during travel and, perhaps most importantly, a crate provides your dog with a place of his own in your home. It serves as a "doggie bedroom" of sorts—your Dachshund can retire in his crate when he wants to sleep or when he just needs a break.

Many dogs sleep in their crates overnight. With soft bedding and a favorite chew toy, a crate becomes a cozy pseudo-den for your dog. Like his ancestors, he too will seek out the comfort and retreat of a den—you just happen to be providing him with something a little more luxurious than what his early ancestors enjoyed.

As far as purchasing a crate, the type that you buy is up to you. It will most likely be one of the two most popular types: wire or fiberglass. There are advantages and disadvantages to each type. For example, a wire crate is more open, allowing the air to flow through and affording the dog a view of what is going on around him while a fiberglass crate is sturdier. Both can double as travel crates, providing protection for the dog.

The size of the crate is another thing to consider. Puppies do not stay puppies forever—in fact, sometimes it seems as if they grow right before your eyes. A medium-size crate will be necessary for a full-grown Dachshund, whose length obviously exceeds his height. Although most dog owners are concerned that the dog will not be able to stand up in his crate, the Dachshund owner must be sure that his dog can stretch out comfortably while in his crate.

Since Dachshund owners must concern themselves with controlling their dogs' exuberance and desire to jump, a crate-trained Dachshund has the advantage of a quiet, familiar place for confinement and "bed rest." A Dachshund is surely better accommodated in his crate for a few hours than left at home unattended, bounding about the furniture and up and down the stairs.

BEDDING

A nice crate pad in the dog's crate will help the dog feel more at home and you may also like to provide a small blanket. This will take the place of the leaves, twigs, etc., that the pup would use in the wild to make a den; the pup can make his own "burrow" in the crate. Although your pup is far removed from

CRATE TRAINING TIPS

During crate training, you should partition off the section of the crate in which the pup stays. If he is given too big an area, this will hinder your training efforts. Crate training is based on the fact that a dog does not like to soil his sleeping quarters, so it is ineffective to keep a pup in a crate that is so big that he can eliminate in one end and get far enough away from it to sleep. Also, you want to make the crate den-like for the pup. Blankets and a favorite toy will make the crate cozy for the small pup; as he

grows, you may want to evict some of his "roommates" to make more room.

It will take some coaxing at first, but be patient. Given some time to get used to it, your Dachshund will adapt to his new home-within-a-home quite nicely.

Wire crates, as well as lightweight fiberglass crates, serve their purpose in that they are light and portable.

In addition to the crate, you should have the dog's bed and a few toys ready for the first night in his new home.

his den-making ancestors, the denning instinct is still a part of his genetic makeup. Also, until you take your pup home, he has been sleeping amid the warmth of his mother and littermates, and while a blanket is not the same as a warm, breathing body, it still provides heat and something with which to snuggle. You will want to wash your pup's bedding frequently in case he has a potty accident in his crate, and replace or remove any blanket that becomes ragged and starts to fall apart.

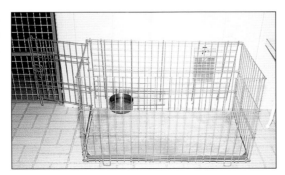

Wire crates are popular for use inside the home.

TOYS

Toys are a must for dogs of all ages, especially for curious playful pups. Puppies are the "children" of the dog world, and what child does not love toys? Chew toys provide enjoyment to both dog and owner—your dog will enjoy playing with his favorite toys, while you will enjoy the fact that they distract him from your expensive shoes and leather couch. Puppies love to chew; in

fact, chewing is a physical need for pups as they are teething, and everything looks appetizing! The full range of your possessions—from old dishrags to the new Oriental rug—are fair game in the eyes of a teething pup. Puppies are not all that discerning when it comes to finding something to literally 'sink their teeth into'—everything tastes great!

Dachshund puppies are aggressive chewers and owners should offer only the hardest, strongest toys available. Breeders advise owners to resist stuffed toys, because they can become de-stuffed in no time. The overly excited pup may ingest the stuffing, which is neither nutritious nor digestible.

Similarly, squeaky toys are quite popular, but must be avoided for the Dachshund. Perhaps a squeaky toy can be used as an aid in training, but not for free play. If a pup "disembowels" one of these, the small plastic squeaker inside can be dangerous if swallowed. Monitor the condition of all your pup's toys carefully and get rid of any that have been chewed to the point of becoming potentially dangerous.

Be careful of natural bones, which have a tendency to splinter into sharp, dangerous pieces. Also be careful of rawhide, which can turn into pieces that are easy to swallow and become a mushy mess on your carpet.

LEASH

A nylon leash is probably the best option, as it is the most resistant to puppy teeth should your pup take a liking to chewing on his leash. Of course,

Toys, Toys, Toys!

With a big variety of dog toys available, and so many that look like they would be a lot of fun for a dog, be careful in your selection. It is amazing what a set of

puppy teeth can do to an innocent-looking toy, so, obviously, safety is a major consideration. Be sure to choose the most durable products that you can find. Hard nylon bones and toys are a safe bet, and many of them are offered in different scents and flavors that will be sure to capture your dog's attention. It is always fun to play a game of catch with your dog, and there are balls and flying discs that are specially made to withstand dog's teeth.

this is a habit that should be nipped in the bud, but, if your pup likes to chew on his leash, he has a very slim chance of being able to chew through the strong nylon. Nylon leashes are also lightweight, which is good for a young Dachshund who is

THE HUNTER AT PLAY

A natural hunter by trade, the Dachshund today retains his prowess in the field to work on small game. Although breeders encourage hunting for their dogs, most Dachshunds today are loving companions and not rabbit hunters. Thus, play not sport becomes the battlecry of the day.

Teaching the puppy to play with his toys in running and fetching games is an ideal way to help the puppy develop muscle, learn motor skills and bond with you, his owner and master. He also needs to learn how to inhibit his bite

reflex and never to use his teeth on people, forbidden objects and other animals in play.

Whenever you play with your puppy, you make the rules. This becomes an important message to your puppy in teaching him that you are the pack leader and control everything he does in life. Once your dog accepts you as his leader, your relationship with him will be cemented for life.

just getting used to the idea of walking on a leash. For everyday walking and safety purposes, the nylon leash is a good choice. As your pup grows up and gets used to walking on the leash, you may want to purchase a flexible leash. These leads allow you to extend the length to give the dog a broader area to explore or to shorten the length to keep the dog closer to you. Of course there are special leashes for training purposes, and specially made harnesses for working dogs, but these are not necessary for routine walks.

COLLAR

Your pup should get used to wearing a collar all the time since you will want to attach his ID tags to it. A lightweight

chew on the steel variety, which can be sterilized. It is important to buy sturdy bowls since anything is in danger of being chewed by puppy teeth and you do not want your dog to be constantly chewing apart his bowl (for his safety and for your wallet!).

Purchase high-quality, durable bowls for your Dachshund.

CLEANING SUPPLIES

Until a pup is house-trained, you will be doing a lot of cleaning. "Accidents" will occur, which is acceptable in the beginning because the puppy does not know any better. All you can do is be prepared to clean up any accidents. Old rags, towels, newspapers and a safe disinfectant are good to have on hand.

nylon collar is a good choice; make sure that it fits snugly enough so that the pup cannot wriggle out of it, but is loose enough so that it will not be uncomfortably tight around the pup's neck. You should be able to fit a finger between the pup and the collar. It may take some time for your pup to get used to wearing the collar, but soon he will not even notice that it is there. Choke collars are made for training, but should only be used by experienced handlers and are not suitable for use on small dogs.

FOOD AND WATER BOWLS

Your pup will need two bowls, one for food and one for water. You may want two sets of bowls, one for inside and one for outside, depending on where the dog will be fed and where he will be spending time. Stainless steel or sturdy plastic bowls are popular choices. Plastic bowls are more chewable. Dogs tend not to

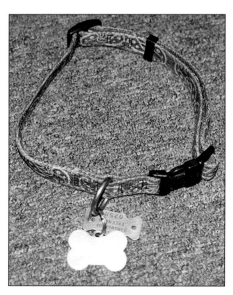

You will need a light yet sturdy everyday collar to which you can attach your Dachshund's identification tags.

Your local pet shop sells an array of dishes and bowls for water and food.

BEYOND THE BASICS
The items previously discussed are the bare necessities. You will find out what else you need as you go along—grooming supplies, flea/tick protection, baby gates to partition a room, etc. These things will vary depending on your situation, but it is important that you have everything you need to feed and make your Dachshund comfortable in his first few days at home.

PUPPY-PROOFING YOUR HOME
Aside from making sure that your Dachshund will be comfortable in your home, you also have to make sure that your home is safe for your

FINANCIAL RESPONSIBILITY

Grooming tools, collars, leashes, crate, dog beds and, of course, toys will be expenses to you when you first obtain your pup, and the cost will continue throughout your dog's lifetime. If your puppy damages or destroys your possessions (as most puppies surely will!) or something belonging to a neighbor, you can calculate additional expense. There is also flea and pest control, which every dog owner faces more than once. You must be able to handle the financial responsibility of owning a dog.

Choose the Appropriate Collar

The **BUCKLE COLLAR** is the standard collar used for everyday purpose. Be sure that you adjust the buckle on growing puppies. Check it every day. It can become too tight overnight! These collars can be made of leather or nylon. Attach your dog's identification tags to this collar.

The **CHOKE COLLAR** is constructed of highly polished steel so that it slides easily through the stainless steel loop. The idea is that the dog controls the pressure around his neck and he will stop pulling if the collar becomes uncomfortable. It should *not* be used on small dogs.

The **HARNESS or HALTER** is for a trained dog that has to be restrained to prevent running away, chasing a cat and the like. Considered the most humane of all devices, it is frequently used on smaller dogs on which collars are not comfortable.

Dachshund

It is your responsibility to clean up after your Dachshund has relieved himself. Pet shops sell various aids to assist in the clean-up task.

Dachshund. This means taking precautions that your pup will not get into anything he should not get into and that there is nothing within his reach that may harm him should he sniff it, chew it, inspect it, etc. This probably seems obvious since, while you are primarily concerned with your pup's safety, at the same time you do not want your belongings to be ruined. Breakables should be placed out of reach if your dog is to have full run of the house. If he is to be limited to certain places within the house, keep any potentially dangerous items in the 'off-limits' areas. An

electrical cord can pose a danger should the puppy decide to taste it—and who is going to convince a pup that it would not make a great chew toy? Cords should be fastened tightly against the wall. If your dog is going to spend time in a crate, make sure that there is nothing near his crate that he can reach if he sticks his curious little nose or paws through the openings. Just as you would with a child, keep all household cleaners and chemicals where the pup cannot reach them.

It is also important to make sure that the outside of your home is safe. Of course your puppy should never be unsupervised, but a pup let loose in the yard will want to run and explore, and he should be granted that freedom. Do not let a fence give you a false sense of security; you would be surprised how crafty (and persistent) a dog can be in

SKULL & CROSSBONES

Thoroughly puppy-proof your house before bringing your puppy home. Never use cockroach or rodent poisons or plant fertilizers in any area accessible to the puppy. Avoid the use of toilet cleaners. Most dogs are born with "toilet-bowl sonar" and will take a drink if the lid is left open. Also keep the trash secured and out of reach.

NATURAL TOXINS

Examine your lawn, flowerbeds and home landscaping before bringing your puppy home. Many varieties of plants have leaves, stems or flowers that are toxic if ingested, and you can depend on a curious puppy to investigate them. Ask your veterinarian for information on poisonous plants or research them at your library.

working out how to dig under and squeeze his way through small holes. The remedy is to make the fence well embedded into the ground, keeping in mind that Dachshunds are professional diggers and can burrow with skill and speed. Be sure to repair or secure any gaps in the fence. Check the fence periodically to ensure that it is in good shape and make repairs

Swimming is ideal exercise for your Dachshund. Introduce your dog to water slowly; you may also have to assist your long-backed pal in entering and exiting the pool. A secure fence around the pool is advised for safety's sake.

SHOW SOME SUPPORT

The Dachshund's body structure calls for careful handling. When picking up a Dachshund, use both hands to support the dog's long back. Place one hand under the chest and the other hand under the hindquarters of the dog.

as needed; a very determined pup may return to the same spot to "work on it" until he is able to get through.

FIRST TRIP TO THE VET
You have picked out your puppy, and your home and family are ready. Now all you have to do is collect your Dachshund from the breeder and the fun begins, right? Well...not so fast. Something else you need to prepare is your pup's first trip to the veterinarian. Perhaps the breeder can recommend someone in the area who specializes in Dachshunds, or maybe you know some other Dachshund owners who can suggest a good vet. Either way, you should have an appointment arranged for your pup before you pick him up.

The pup's first visit will consist of an overall examination to make sure that the pup does not have any problems that are not apparent to you. The veterinarian will also set up a schedule for the pup's vaccinations; the breeder will inform you of which ones the pup has already received and the vet can continue from there.

**INTRODUCTION
TO THE FAMILY**
Everyone in the house will be excited about the puppy's coming home and will want to

pet him and play with him, but it is best to make the introduction low-key so as not to overwhelm the puppy. He is apprehensive already. It is the first time he has been separated from his mother and the breeder, and the ride to your home is likely to be the first time he has been in a car. The last thing you want to do is smother him, as this will only frighten him further. This is not to say that human contact is not extremely necessary at this stage, because this is the time when a connection between the pup and his human family is formed. Gentle petting and soothing words should help console him, as well as just putting him down and letting him explore on his own (under your watchful eye, of course).

Dachshunds and children make natural friends. Dachshunds appreciate how close to the ground children are and enjoy their company.

THE RIDE HOME

Taking your dog from the breeder to your home in a car can be a very uncomfortable experience for both of you. The puppy will have been taken from his warm, friendly, safe environment and brought into a strange new environment—an environment that moves! Be reassuring to the pup during the ride. Be prepared for loose bowels, urination, crying, whining and even fear biting. With proper love and encouragement when you arrive home, the stress of the trip should quickly disappear.

The pup may approach the family members or may busy himself with exploring for a while. Gradually, each person should spend some time with the pup, one at a time, crouching down to get as close to the pup's level as possible and letting him sniff their hands and petting him gently. He definitely needs human attention and he needs to be touched—this is how to form an immediate bond. Just remember that the pup is experiencing a lot of things for the first time, at the same time. There are new people, new noises, new smells and new things to investigate, so be gentle, be affectionate and be as comforting as you can be.

TOXIC PLANTS

Many plants can be toxic to dogs. If you see your dog carrying a piece of vegetation in his mouth, approach him in a quiet, disinterested manner, avoid eye contact, pet him and gradually remove the plant from his mouth. Alternatively, offer him a treat and maybe he'll drop the plant on his own accord. Be sure no toxic plants are growing anywhere in your own yard or garden.

PUP'S FIRST NIGHT HOME

You have traveled home with your new charge safely in his crate. He's been to the vet for a thorough check-up, he's been weighed, his papers examined; perhaps he's even been vaccinated and wormed as

Be sure that your new Dachshund meets the whole family. Socialization is an important part of dog training.

well. He's met the family and he's licked the whole family, including the excited children and the less-than-happy cat. He's explored his area, his new bed, the yard and anywhere else he's been permitted. He's eaten his first meal at home and relieved himself in the proper place. He's heard lots of new sounds, smelled new friends and seen more of the outside world than ever before.

That was just the first day! He's worn out and is ready for bed…or so you think!

It's puppy's first night and you are ready to say "Good night"—keep in mind that this is puppy's first night ever to be sleeping alone. His dam and littermates are no longer at paw's length and he's a bit scared, cold and lonely. Be reassuring to your new family member. This is not the time to spoil him and give in to his inevitable whining.

Puppies whine. They whine to let others know where they are and hopefully to get company out of it. Place your pup in his new bed or crate in his room and close the door. Mercifully, he may fall asleep without a peep. If the inevitable occurs, ignore the whining; he is fine. Be strong and keep his best interest in mind. Do not allow yourself to feel guilty and visit the pup.

PUPPY FEEDING

You will probably start feeding your pup the same food that he has been getting from the breeder; the breeder should give you a few days' supply to start you off. Although you should not give your pup too many treats, you will want to have puppy treats on hand for coaxing, training, rewards, etc. Be careful, though, as a small pup's calorie requirements are relatively low and a few treats can add up to almost a full day's worth of calories without the required nutrition.

He will fall asleep eventually.

Many breeders recommend placing a piece of bedding from his former home in his new bed so that he recognizes the scent of his littermates. Others still advise placing a hot water bottle in his bed for warmth. The latter may be a good idea provided the pup doesn't attempt to suckle—he'll get good and wet and may not fall asleep so fast.

Puppy's first night

can be somewhat stressful for the pup and his new family. Remember that you are setting the tone of nighttime at your house. Unless you want to play with your pup every night at 10 p.m., midnight and 2 a.m., don't initiate the habit. Your family will thank you, and so will your pup!

PREVENTING PUPPY PROBLEMS

SOCIALIZATION
Now that you have done all of the preparatory work and have helped your pup get accustomed to his new home and family, it is about time for you to have some fun! Socializing your Dachshund pup gives you

This priceless eight-week-old arrived with a towel from the breeder's home, so that the pup would have a familiar object while settling in with her new owners.

61

the opportunity to show off your new friend, and your pup gets to reap the benefits of being an adorable little creature that people will want to pet and, in general, think is absolutely precious!

Besides getting to know his new family, your puppy should be exposed to other people, animals and situations, but of course he must not come into close contact with dogs you don't know well until his course of injections is fully complete. This will help him become well adjusted as he grows up and less prone to being timid or fearful of the new things he will encounter. Your pup's socialization began at the breeder's, but now it is your responsibility to continue

MANNERS MATTER

During the socialization process, a puppy should meet people, experience different environments and definitely be exposed to other canines. Through playing and interacting with other dogs, your puppy will learn lessons, ranging from controlling the pressure of his jaws by biting his littermates to the inner-workings of the canine pack that he will apply to his human relationships for the rest of his life. That is why removing a puppy from its litter too early (before eight weeks) can be detrimental to the pup's development, as much early socialization occurs before the pup leaves the breeder.

it. The socialization he receives up until the age of 12 weeks is the most critical, as this is the time when he forms his impres-

Pepsi, a Smooth Miniature Dachshund, gets along famously with housemate Bourke, a Siamese cat. The new Dachshund should be carefully introduced to the other animals in the household. Owner, Terri McCready.

SOCIALIZATION PERIOD

The socialization period for puppies is from age 8 to 16 weeks. This is the time when puppies need to leave their birth family and take up residence with their new owners, where they will meet many new people, other pets, etc. Failure to be adequately socialized can cause the dog to grow up fearing others and being shy and unfriendly due to a lack of self-confidence. Of course, careful introductions should be made anytime your pup meets a new person or animal.

Thorough socialization includes not only meeting new people but also being introduced to new experiences such as riding in the car, having his coat brushed, hearing the television, walking in a crowd—the list is endless. The more your pup experiences, and the more positive the experiences are, the less of a shock and the less frightening it will be for your pup to encounter new things, and the better adjusted he will be as an adult.

sions of the outside world. Be especially careful during the eight-to-ten-week period, also known as the fear period. The interaction he receives during this time should be gentle and reassuring. Lack of socialization can manifest itself in fear and aggression as the dog grows up. The pup needs lots of human contact, affection, handling and exposure to other animals.

Once your pup has received his necessary vaccinations, feel free to take him out and about (on his leash, of course). Walk him around the neighborhood, take him on your daily errands, let people pet him, let him meet other dogs and pets, etc. Puppies do not have to try to make friends; there will be no

Who can resist the fond lick of a handsome Dachshund?

THE COCOA WARS

Chocolate contains the chemical bromine, which is poisonous to dogs. You also should be cautious when using mulch in your yard. This frequently contains cocoa hulls, and dogs have been known to die from eating mulch.

pup that has a bad experience with a child may grow up to be a dog that is shy around or aggressive toward children.

CONSISTENCY IN TRAINING

Dogs, being pack animals, naturally need a leader, or else they try to establish dominance in their packs. When you bring a dog into your family, the choice of who becomes the leader and who becomes the "pack" is entirely up to you! Your pup's intuitive quest for dominance, coupled with the fact that it is nearly impossible to look at an adorable Dachshund pup with his "puppy-dog" eyes and not cave in, give the pup almost an unfair advantage in getting the upper hand! A pup will definitely test the waters to see what he can and cannot do. Do not give in to those pleading eyes—stand your ground when it comes to disciplining the pup and make sure that all family members do the same. It will only confuse the pup when Mom tells him to get off the couch when he is used to sitting up there with Dad to watch the nightly news. Avoid discrepancies by having all members of the household decide on the rules before the pup even comes home...and be consistent in enforcing them! Early training shapes the dog's personality, so

shortage of people who will want to introduce themselves. Just make sure that you carefully supervise each meeting. If the neighborhood children want to say hello, for example, that is great—children and pups most often make great companions. Sometimes an excited child can unintentionally handle a pup too roughly, or an overzealous pup can playfully nip a little too hard. You want to make socialization experiences positive ones. What a pup learns during this very formative stage will affect his attitude toward future encounters. You want your dog to be comfortable around everyone. A

Even though the Dachshund comes in chocolate, this tempting treat must be avoided.

64

TRAINING TIP

Training your Dachshund takes much patience and can be frustrating at times, but you should see results from your efforts. If you have a dog that seems untrainable, take him to a

trainer or behaviorist. The dog may have a personality problem that requires the help of a professional, or perhaps you need help in learning how to train your dog.

you cannot be unclear in what you expect.

COMMON PUPPY PROBLEMS

The best way to prevent puppy problems is to be proactive in stopping an undesirable behavior as soon as it starts. The old saying "You can't teach an old dog new tricks" does not necessarily hold true, but it is true that it is much easier to discourage bad behavior in a young developing pup than to wait until the pup's bad behavior becomes the adult dog's bad habit. There are some problems that are especially prevalent in puppies as they develop.

NIPPING

As puppies start to teethe, they feel the need to sink their teeth into anything available...unfortunately that can include your fingers, arms, hair and toes. You may find this behavior cute for the first five seconds...until you feel just how sharp those puppy teeth are. This is something you want to discourage immediately and consistently with a firm "No!" (or whatever number of firm "Nos" it takes for him to understand that you mean business). Then replace your finger with an appropriate chew toy. While this behavior is merely annoying when the dog is young, it can become dangerous as your Dachshund's adult teeth grow in

65

and his jaws develop, and he continues to think it is okay to gnaw on human appendages. Your Dachshund does not mean any harm with a friendly nip, but he also does not know his own strength.

CRYING/WHINING
Your pup will often cry, whine, whimper, howl or make some type of commotion when he is left alone. This is basically his way of calling out for attention to make sure that you know he is there and that you have not forgotten about him. He feels insecure when he is left alone, when you are out of the house and he is in his crate or when you are in another part of the house and he cannot see you. The noise he is making is an expression of the anxiety he feels at being alone, so he needs to be taught that being alone is okay. You are not actually training the dog to stop making noise, you are training him to feel comfortable when he is alone and thus removing the need for him to make the noise.

This is where the crate with cozy bedding and a toy comes in handy. You want to know that he is safe when you are not there to supervise, and you know that he will be safe in his crate rather than roaming freely about the house. In order for the pup to stay in his crate without making

a fuss, he needs to be comfortable in his crate. On that note, it is extremely important that the crate is never used as a form of punishment, or the pup will have a negative association with the crate.

Accustom the pup to the crate in short, gradually increasing time intervals in which you put him in the crate, maybe with a treat, and stay in the room with him. If he cries or makes a fuss, do not go to him, but stay in his sight. Gradually he will realize that staying in his crate is all right without your help, and it will not be so traumatic for him when you are not around. You may want to leave the radio on softly when you leave the house; the sound of human voices may be comforting to him.

CHEWING TIP

Chewing goes hand in hand with nipping in the sense that a teething puppy is always looking for a way to soothe his aching gums. In this case, instead of chewing on you, he may have taken a liking to your favorite shoe or something else which he should not be chewing. Again, realize that this is a normal canine behavior that does not need to be discouraged, only redirected. Your pup just needs to be taught what is acceptable to chew on and what is off-limits.

A safe chew toy, like a sturdy ball, is ideal for the Dachshund puppy. Always supervise your puppy whenever he is playing with a new toy.

TIPPING THE SCALES

Good nutrition is vital to your dog's health, but many people end up over-feeding or giving unnecessary supplements. Here are some common doggie diet don'ts:

- Adding milk, yogurt and cheese to your dog's diet may seem like a good idea for coat and skin care, but dairy products are very fattening and can cause indigestion.
- Diets high in fat will not cause heart attacks in dogs but will certainly cause your dog to gain weight.
- Most importantly, don't assume your dog will simply stop eating once he doesn't need any more food. Given the chance, he will eat you out of house and home!

DIETARY AND FEEDING CONSIDERATIONS

Today, the choices of food for your Dachshund are many and varied. There are simply dozens of brands of food in all sorts of flavors and textures, ranging from puppy diets to those for seniors. There are even hypoallergenic and low-calorie diets available. Because your Dachshund's food has a bearing on coat, health and temperament, it is essential that the most suitable diet is selected for a Dachshund of his age. It is fair to say, however, that even experienced owners can be perplexed by the enormous range of foods available. Only understanding what is best for your dog will help you reach an informed decision.

Dog foods are produced in three basic types: dry, semi-moist and canned. Dry foods are useful for the cost-conscious, for overall they tend to be less expensive than semi-moist or canned. They also contain the least fat and the most preservatives. In general, canned foods are made up of 60–70 percent water, while semi-moist ones often contain so much sugar that they are perhaps the least preferred by owners, even though their dogs seem to like them.

When selecting your dog's diet, three stages of development must be considered: the puppy stage, the adult stage and the senior stage.

PUPPY STAGE

Puppies instinctively want to suck milk from their mother's teats and a normal puppy will exhibit this behavior from just a few moments following birth. If puppies do not attempt to suckle within the first half-hour or so, they should be encouraged to do so by placing them on the nipples, having selected ones with plenty of milk. This early milk supply is important in providing colostrum to protect the puppies during the first eight to ten weeks of their lives. Although mother's milk is much better than any milk formula, despite there being some excellent ones available, if the puppies do not feed, the breeder will have to feed them himself. For those with less experience, advice from a veterinarian is important so that not only the right quantity of milk is fed but also that of correct quality, fed at suitably frequent intervals, usually every two hours during the first few days of life.

FOOD PREFERENCE

Selecting the best dry dog food is difficult. There is no majority consensus among veterinary scientists as to the value of nutrient analysis (protein, fat, fiber,

moisture, ash, cholesterol, minerals, etc.). All agree that feeding trials are what matter, but you also have to consider the individual dog. The dog's weight, age and activity level, and what pleases his taste, all must be considered. It is probably best to take the advice of your veterinarian. Every dog's dietary requirements vary, even during the lifetime of a particular dog.

If your dog is fed a good dry food, it does not require supplements of meat or vegetables. Dogs do appreciate a little variety in their diets, so you may choose to stay with the same brand but vary the flavor. Alternatively, you may wish to add a little flavored stock to give a difference to the taste.

Vitamin and mineral supplementation also should not be necessary if feeding a complete dog food. Supplements only should be added under your vet's advisement.

Dachshund

Your Dachshund's health is evident in his eyes, coat and behavior. An adult's proper nutrition affects all these as well as his weight and overall condition.

meals will be reduced over time, and when a young dog has reached the age of about 10 to 12 months, he should be switched to an adult diet.

Puppy and junior diets can be well balanced for the needs of your dog so that, except in certain circumstances, additional vitamins, minerals and proteins will not be required.

ADULT DIETS

A dog is considered an adult when it has stopped growing, so in general the diet of a Dachshund can be changed to an adult one at about 10 to 12 months of age. Again you should rely upon your veterinarian or dietary specialist to recommend an acceptable maintenance diet. Major dog food manufacturers specialize in

Puppies should be allowed to nurse from their mothers for about the first six weeks, although from the third or fourth week the breeder will begin to introduce small portions of suitable solid food. Most breeders like to introduce alternate milk and meat meals initially, building up to weaning time.

By the time the puppies are seven or a maximum of eight weeks old, they should be fully weaned and fed solely on a proprietary puppy food. Selection of the most suitable, good-quality diet at this time is essential, for a puppy's fastest growth rate is during the first year of life. Veterinarians are usually able to offer advice in this regard. The frequency of

STORING DOG FOOD

You must store your dry dog food carefully. Open packages of dog food quickly lose their vitamin value, usually within 90 days of being opened. Mold spores and vermin could also contaminate the food.

70

this type of food, and it is merely necessary for you to select the one best suited to your dog's needs.

Since Dachshunds are more prone to obesity than many other breeds of dog, owners must monitor their Dachshunds' diets with special care. Neutered Dachshunds are twice as prone to obesity as unaltered dogs and should be fed a reduced-calorie food, especially designed for the obesity-prone. Owners should consider not leaving the Dachshund's food out all day for "free-choice" feeding, as this freedom inevitably translates to inches around the Dachshund's waist.

SENIOR DIETS

As dogs get older, their metabolism changes. The older dog usually exercises less, moves more slowly and sleeps more. This change in lifestyle and physiological performance requires a change in diet. Since these changes take place slowly, they might not be recognizable. These metabolic changes increase the tendency toward obesity, requiring an even more vigilant approach to feeding. Obesity in an older dog compounds the health problems that already accompany old age.

As your dog gets older, few of his organs function up to par. The kidneys slow down and the intestines become less efficient. These age-related factors are best handled with a change in diet and a change in feeding schedule to give smaller portions that are more easily digested.

There is no single best diet for every older dog. While many dogs do well on light or senior diets, other dogs do better on puppy diets or other special premium diets such as lamb and rice. Be sensitive to your senior Dachshund's diet and this will help control other problems that may arise with your old friend.

DO DOGS HAVE TASTE BUDS?

Watching a dog "wolf" or gobble his food, seemingly without chewing, leads an owner to wonder whether his dog can taste anything. Yes, dogs have taste buds, with sensory perception of sweet, salty and sour. Puppies are born with fully mature taste buds.

71

CHANGE IN DIET

As your dog's caretaker, you know the importance of keeping his diet consistent, but sometimes when you run out of food or if you're away, you'll need to change quickly. Some dogs will experience digestive problems, but most will not. If you are planning on changing your dog's menu, do so gradually to ensure that your dog will not have any problems. Over a period of four to five days, slowly add some new food to your dog's old food, increasing the percentage of new food each day.

Water is absolutely essential to dogs, and it must be available at all times. Monitor the amount of water your puppy drinks during housebreaking so that you will know when he'll need to relieve himself.

WATER

Just as your dog needs proper nutrition from his food, water is an essential "nutrient" as well. Water keeps the dog's body properly hydrated and promotes normal function of the body's systems. During housebreaking, it is necessary to keep an eye on how much water your Dachshund is drinking, but once he is reliably trained he should have access to clean fresh water at all times, especially if you feed dry food. Make sure that the dog's water bowl is clean, and change the water often.

EXERCISE

Dachshunds are hardy little dogs, capable of running down badgers and hares and burrowing into tunnels with great endurance. However, most Dachshunds live much more quiet lives, with their exercise limited to what they do with their owners and families. How they must miss the excitement of chasing a badger down a hole!

It would not be wise to let your Dachshund sit home alone all week while you're at work and then try to exercise the dog in the great outdoors on the weekend. To enjoy and benefit from physical exercise, dogs must enjoy that exercise on a regular basis. One day a week is insufficient to create a fit dog—

DRINK, DRANK, DRUNK— MAKE IT A DOUBLE

In both humans and dogs, as well as all other living organisms, water forms the major part of nearly every body tissue. Naturally, we take water for granted, but without it, life as we know it would cease.

For dogs, water is needed to keep their bodies functioning biochemically. Additionally, water is needed to replace the water lost while panting. Unlike humans, who are able to sweat to dissipate heat, dogs must pant to cool down, thereby losing the vital water from their bodies needed to regulate their body temperatures. Humans lose electrolyte-containing products and other body-fluid components through sweating; dogs do not lose anything except water.

Water is essential always, but especially so when the weather is hot or humid or when your dog is exercising or working vigorously.

Dachshunds are active, enthusiastic and up for almost anything—even a romp on the beach or a dip in the ocean!

"DOES THIS COLLAR MAKE ME LOOK FAT?"

While humans may obsess about their own weight, many people believe that extra weight on their dogs is a good thing. The truth is, pets should not be over- or under-weight, as both can lead to or signal sickness. In order to tell how fit your pet is, run your hands over his ribs. Are his ribs buried under a layer of fat or are they sticking out considerably? If your pet is within his normal weight range, you should be able to feel the ribs easily, but they should not protrude abnormally. If you stand above him, the outline of his body should resemble an hourglass. Some breeds do tend to be leaner while some are a bit stockier, but making sure your dog is the right weight for his breed will certainly contribute to his good health.

or human!

Walking is just as beneficial for dogs as it is for humans. Thus, a brisk walk of a reasonable distance is still the best possible way to exercise lungs and limbs. Moreover, the human walker will also reap the benefits of regular exercise.

Fetching games in which the dog runs after items such as a ball or frisbee are also excellent ways to exercise. As you begin teaching your puppy to fetch, remember that he's a predator at heart and he instinctively loves to chase things. A ball, to him, is just as exciting as a rabbit, providing that it's moving and he can catch it. Be sure to praise lavishly when he does, so he will be anxious to do it again and again.

A simple recipe for having and maintaining a healthy Dachshund is to keep him slim and well exercised.

GROOMING

A minimum amount of grooming is all that is required for Dachshunds. For the

A Worthy Investment

**Veterinary studies have proven that a balanced high-quality diet
pays off in your dog's coat quality, behavior and activity level.
Invest in premium brands for the maximum payoff with your dog.**

Treats are useful in encouraging correct behavior, such as standing for grooming or nail trimming. With a Dachshund, the power of food is endless.

Smooth, a grooming glove with hair bristles can be run over the dog weekly to remove dead hair and restore the shine to the coat.

Longhaireds and Wire-haireds can be brushed weekly to keep their coats free of dirt and debris and to maintain healthy skin.

Your veterinarian can teach you how to brush your dog's teeth. This should be started from puppyhood; you can obtain the necessary supplies from the vet's office at the same time that you receive instruction in dental hygiene. Dental care for the Dachshund is so very important, as the breed tends to be prone to certain congenital dental problems.

BATHING

Dachshunds don't need to be bathed often, providing that they are brushed on a regular schedule. Several times a year and whenever your dog gets into something that creates an unpleasant odor, he can be washed, using a dog shampoo. Human shampoo dries out the hair too much and can cause skin problems in dogs.

Brush your Dachshund thoroughly before wetting his coat. For the Smooth, this will remove any loose dirt from his coat. For the Long and Wire, brushing will get rid of most mats and tangles, which are

GROOMING EQUIPMENT

How much grooming equipment you purchase will depend on how much grooming you are going to do. Here are some basics:
- Natural bristle brush
- Slicker brush
- Metal comb
- Grooming glove
- Rubber mat
- Dog shampoo
- Spray hose attachment
- Blow dryer
- Towels
- Ear cleaner
- Cotton wipes
- Nail clippers
- Toothbrush and canine toothpaste

harder to remove when the coat is wet. Make certain that your dog has a good non-slip surface on which to stand.

Begin by wetting the dog's coat. A shower or hose attachment is necessary for thoroughly wetting and rinsing the coat. Check the water temperature to make sure that it is neither too hot nor too cold. Wet the dog with warm water, then apply the shampoo and rub it into a lather just as you do when you shampoo your own hair. Wash the head last; you do not want shampoo to drip into the dog's eyes while you are washing the rest of his body. Work the shampoo all the way down to the skin. You can use this opportunity to check the skin for any bumps, bites or other abnormalities. Do not neglect any area of the body—get all of the hard-to-reach places.

Rinse thoroughly with warm water to remove all soap. Protect the dog's eyes from the shampoo by shielding them with your hand and directing the flow of water in the opposite direction. You should also avoid getting water in the ear canal. Leaving a residue of chemicals can cause major harm to hair and skin, so be certain that the dog is well rinsed. Be prepared for your dog to shake out his coat—you

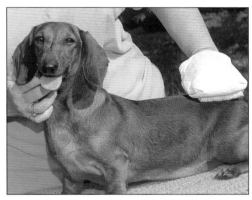

might want to stand back, but make sure you have a hold on the dog to keep him from running through the house.

Towel-dry the coat after the final rinsing. Following that, you can air-dry the coat, but you must keep the dog out of the cold air and drafts until he is completely dry. You may choose to dry the coat with a blow dryer, in which case you'll find that the dog dries much more quickly.

EAR CLEANING
While you're in the process of washing your Dachshund, lift

A grooming glove is recommended for keeping a Smooth's coat lustrous and healthy.

Longhaired and Wirehaired Dachshunds need slightly more grooming care than do Smooth Dachshunds. Whatever your variety, a knowledgeable pet shop employee can assist you in the proper selection of grooming equipment.

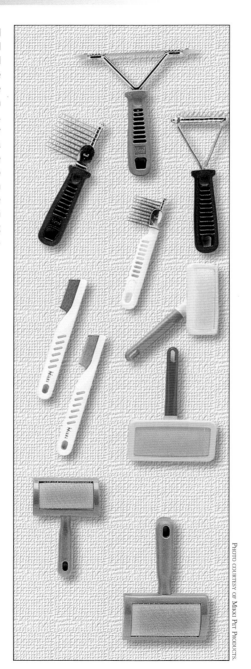

PHOTO COURTESY OF MIKKI PET PRODUCTS.

each ear flap and gently wipe the inside of the ears with a damp face cloth. The ears should be kept clean and any excess hair inside the ear should be carefully plucked out. Ears can be cleaned with a cotton ball and ear powder made especially for dogs. Never force your finger or any object down into the deeper part of the ear. Wipe only the surface you can see and touch easily. Any further cleaning must be performed by your vet.

Be on the lookout for any signs of infection or ear-mite infestation. If your Dachshund has been shaking his head or scratching at his ears frequently, this usually indicates a problem. If his ears have an unusual odor, this is a sure sign of mite infestation or infection, and a signal to have his ears checked by the veterinarian.

SOAP IT UP

The use of human soap products like shampoo, bubble bath and hand soap can be damaging to a dog's coat and skin. Human products are too strong; they remove the protective oils coating the dog's hair and skin that make him water-resistant. Use only shampoo made especially for dogs. You may like to use a medicated shampoo, which will help to keep external parasites at bay.

NAIL CLIPPING

Periodic nail trimming can be done during the brushing routine. Your veterinarian will teach you how to cut your dog's nails without cutting the "quick." The hunting Dachshund, an expert at digging, will need longer nails than his cousin who lives and plays at home.

Your Dachshund should be accustomed to having his nails trimmed at an early age, since it will be part of your maintenance routine throughout his life. Not only does it look nicer, but long nails can scratch someone unintentionally. Also, a long nail has a better chance of

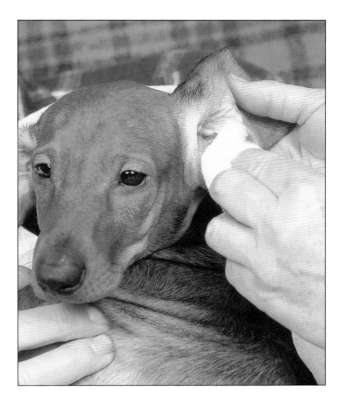

BATHING BEAUTY

Once you are sure that the dog is thoroughly rinsed, squeeze the excess water out of his coat with your hand and dry him with a heavy towel. You may choose to use a blow dryer on his coat or just let it dry naturally. In cold weather, never allow your dog outside with a wet coat.

There are "dry bath" products on the market, which are sprays and powders intended for spot cleaning, that can be used between regular baths if necessary. They are not substitutes for regular baths, but they are easy to use for touch-ups as they do not require rinsing.

ripping and bleeding, or causing the feet to spread. A good rule of thumb is that if you can hear your dog's nails' clicking on the floor when he walks, his nails are too long.

Before you start cutting, make sure you can identify the "quick" in each nail. The quick is a blood vessel that runs through the center of each nail and grows rather close to the end. It will bleed if accidentally cut, which will be quite painful for the dog as it contains nerve endings. Keep some type of

Don't forget the Dachshund's ears. The long ears need careful cleaning on a regular basis and an examination to ascertain that they are mite-free.

The Dachshund accustomed to having his nails clipped will be calm and patient during his pedicure.

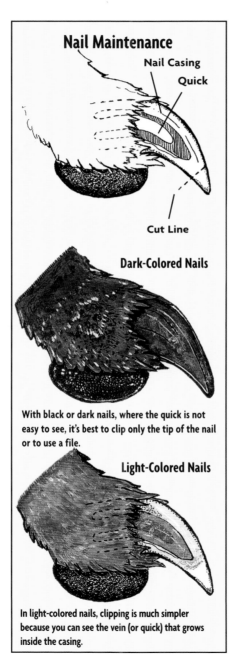

Nail Maintenance

Nail Casing

Quick

Cut Line

Dark-Colored Nails

With black or dark nails, where the quick is not easy to see, it's best to clip only the tip of the nail or to use a file.

Light-Colored Nails

In light-colored nails, clipping is much simpler because you can see the vein (or quick) that grows inside the casing.

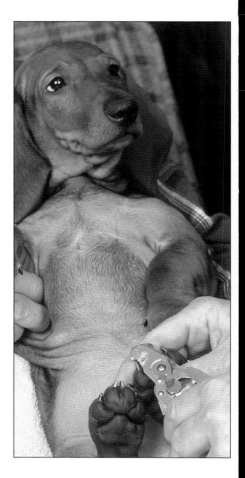

clotting agent on hand, such as a styptic pencil or styptic powder (the type used for shaving). This will stop the bleeding quickly when applied to the end of the cut nail. Do not panic if this happens, just stop the bleeding and talk soothingly to your dog. Once he has calmed down, move on to the next nail. It is better to clip

PEDICURE TIP

A dog that spends a lot of time outside on a hard surface, such as cement or pavement, will have his nails naturally worn down and may not need to have them trimmed as often, except maybe in the colder months when he is not outside as much. Regardless, it is best to

get your dog accustomed to the nail-trimming procedure at an early age so that he is used to it. Some dogs are especially sensitive about having their feet touched, but if a dog has experienced it since puppyhood, it should not bother him.

a little at a time, particularly with black-nailed dogs.

Hold your pup steady as you begin trimming his nails; you do not want him to make any sudden movements or run away. Talk to him soothingly and stroke him as you clip. Holding his foot in your hand, simply take off the end of each nail in one quick clip. You can purchase nail clippers that are specially made for dogs; you can probably find them wherever you buy grooming supplies.

If your Dachshund is acclimated to the nail clipping process, he will usually stand quietly during the procedure.

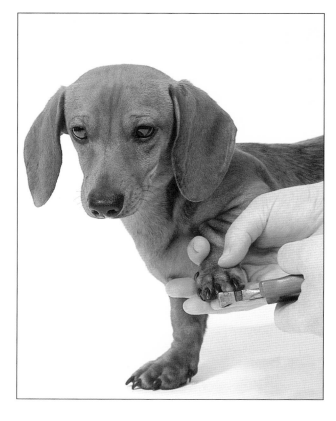

TRAVEL TIP

Never leave your dog alone in the car. In hot weather, your dog can die from the high temperature inside a closed vehicle; even a car parked in the shade can heat up very quickly. Leaving the window open is dangerous as well since the dog can hurt himself trying to get out.

TRAVELING WITH YOUR DOG

CAR TRAVEL

You should accustom your Dachshund to riding in a car at an early age. You may or may not take him in the car often, but at the very least he will need to go to the vet and you do not want these trips to be traumatic for the dog or troublesome for you. The safest way for a dog to ride in the car is in his crate. If he uses a crate in the house, you can use the same crate for travel.

Put the pup in the crate and see how he reacts. If he seems uneasy, you can have a passenger hold him on his lap while you drive. Another option is a specially made safety harness for dogs, which straps the dog in much like a seat belt. Do not let the dog roam loose in the vehicle—this is very dangerous! If you should stop short, your dog can be thrown and injured. If the dog starts climbing on you and pestering you while you are driving, you will not be able to concentrate on the road. It is an unsafe situation for everyone—human and canine.

For long trips, be prepared to stop to let the dog relieve himself. Take with you whatever you need to clean up after him, including some paper towels and perhaps some old bath towels for use should he have an accident in the car or suffer from motion sickness.

AIR TRAVEL

Contact your chosen airline before proceeding with your travel plans that include your Dachshund. The dog will be required to travel in a fiberglass crate and you should always check in advance with the airline regarding specific requirements. On many airlines, small pets whose crates fall within the specified size limita-

ON THE RUN

When traveling, never let your dog off-lead in a strange area. Your dog could run away out of fear, decide to chase a passing squirrel or cat or simply want to stretch his legs without restriction—if any of these happen, you might never see your canine friend again.

tions are granted "carry-on" status and can accompany their owners in the cabin (but must stay in their crates). This may be possible with a Mini; again, check with the airline ahead of time.

To help put the dog at ease, give him one of his favorite toys in the crate. Do not feed the dog for several hours prior to checking in so that you minimize his need to relieve himself. For long trips, you will have to include food and water bowls in the dog's crate, and a portion of food, as airline employees will tend to the dogs during any stops.

Make sure your dog is properly identified and that your contact information appears on his ID tags and on his crate. If not permitted in the cabin, your Dachshund will travel in a different area of the plane than human passengers, so every rule must be strictly followed to prevent the risk of getting separated from your dog.

BOARDING

So you want to take a family vacation—and you want to include *all* members of the family. You would probably make arrangements for accommodations ahead of time anyway, but this is especially important when traveling with a dog. You do not want to make an overnight stop at the only place around for miles and find out that they do not allow

Air travel is never as simple as this. This Dachshund's owners have reserved the whole plane for her special vacation.

GOING ABROAD

For international travel, you will have to make arrangements well in advance (perhaps months), as countries' regulations pertaining to bringing in animals differ. There may be special health certificates and/or vaccinations that your dog will need before taking the trip; sometimes this has to be done within a certain time frame. When traveling to rabies-free countries, you will need to bring proof of the dog's rabies vaccination and there will likely be a quarantine period upon arrival.

dogs. Also, you do not want to reserve a room for your family without confirming that you are traveling with a dog because, if it is against their policy, you may not have a place to stay.

Alternatively, if you are traveling and choose not to bring your Dachshund, you will have to make arrangements for him. Some options are to bring him to a neighbor's house, to have a trusted neighbor stop by often or stay at your house or to bring your

A satisfactory boarding kennel should be located before you actually need it. The kennel should be clean and neat. The runs should be large enough so that the dog can exercise properly.

dog to a reputable boarding kennel. If you choose to board him at a kennel, you should visit in advance to see the facilities provided, how clean they are and where the dogs are kept. Talk to some of the employees and see how they treat the dogs—do they spend time with the dogs, play with them, exercise them, etc.? Also find out the kennel's policy on vaccinations and what they require. This is for all of the dogs' safety since, when dogs are kept together, there is a greater risk of diseases being passed from dog to dog.

IDENTIFICATION

Your Dachshund is your valued companion and friend. That is why you always keep a close eye on him and you have made sure that he cannot escape from the yard or wriggle out of his collar and run away from you. However, accidents can happen and there may come a time when your dog unexpectedly gets separated from you. If this unfortunate event should occur, the first thing on your mind will be finding him. Proper identification, including an ID tag, a tattoo and possibly a microchip, will increase the chances of his being returned to you safely and quickly.

IDENTIFICATION

As puppies become more and more expensive, especially those puppies of high quality for showing and/or breeding, they have a greater chance of being stolen. The usual collar dog tag is, of course, easily removed. But there are two permanent techniques that have become widely used for identification.

The puppy microchip implantation involves the injection of a small microchip, about the size of a corn kernel, under the skin of the dog. If your dog shows up at a clinic or shelter, or is offered for resale under less-than-savory circumstances, it can be positively identified by the microchip. The microchip is scanned, and a registry quickly identifies you as the owner.

Tattooing is done on various parts of the dog, from his belly to his cheeks. The number tattooed can be your dog's AKC registration number or any other number that you can easily memorize. When professional dog thieves see a tattooed dog, they usually lose interest. Both microchipping and tattooing can be done at your local veterinary clinic. For the safety of our dogs, no laboratory facility or dog broker will accept a tattooed dog as stock.

Discuss microchipping and tattooing with your vet and breeder. Some vets and breeders perform these services on their own premises for a reasonable fee. Be certain that the dog is then properly registered with a national database.

Living with an untrained dog is a lot like owning a piano that you do not know how to play—it is a nice object to look at, but it does not do much more than that to bring you pleasure. Now try taking piano lessons, and suddenly the piano comes alive and brings forth magical sounds and rhythms that set your heart singing and your body swaying.

The same is true with your Dachshund. Any dog is a big responsibility and, if not trained sensibly, may develop unacceptable behavior that annoys you or could even cause family friction.

To train your Dachshund, you may like to enroll in an obedience class. Teach him good manners as you learn how and why he behaves the way he does. Find out how to communicate with your dog and how to recognize and understand his communications with you. Suddenly the dog takes on a new role in your life—he is clever, interesting, well-behaved and fun to be with. He demonstrates his bond of devotion to you daily. In

REAP THE REWARDS

If you start with a normal, healthy dog and give him time, patience and some carefully executed lessons, you will reap the rewards of that training for the life of the dog. And what a life it will be! The two of you will find immeasurable pleasure in the companionship you have built together with love, respect and understanding.

other words, your Dachshund does wonders for your ego because he constantly reminds you that you are not only his leader, you are his hero!

Those involved with teaching dog obedience and counseling owners about their dogs' behavior have discovered some interesting facts about dog ownership. For example, training dogs when they are puppies results in the highest rate of success in developing well-mannered and well-adjusted adult dogs. Training an older dog, from six months to six years of age, can produce almost equal results, providing that the owner accepts the dog's slower rate of learning capability and is willing to work patiently to help the dog succeed at developing to his fullest potential. Unfortunately, many owners of untrained adult dogs lack the patience factor, so they do not persist until their dogs are successful at learning particular behaviors.

Training a puppy aged 10 to 16 weeks (20 weeks at the most) is like working with a dry sponge in a pool of water. The pup soaks up whatever you show him and constantly looks for more things to do and learn. At this early age, his body is not yet producing hormones, and therein lies the reason for such a high rate of success. Without hormones, he is focused on his owners and not particularly interested in investigating other places, dogs, people, etc. You are his leader: his provider of food, water, shelter and security. He latches on to you and wants to stay close. He will usually follow you from room to room, will not let you out of his sight when you are outdoors with him and will respond in like manner to the people and animals you encounter. If you greet a friend warmly, he will be happy to greet the person as well. If, however, you are hesitant or anxious about the approach of a stranger, he will respond accordingly.

Once the puppy begins to produce hormones, his natural curiosity

PARENTAL GUIDANCE

Training a dog is a life experience. Many parents admit that much of what they know about raising children they learned from caring for their dogs. Just as children look to their parents for love, fairness and guidance, dogs look to their human owners for the same. Become a good dog owner and you may become an even better parent.

87

MEALTIME

Mealtime should be a peaceful time for your Dachshund. Do not put your dog's food and water bowls in a high-traffic area in the house. For example, give him his own little corner of the kitchen where he can eat undisturbed and where he will not be underfoot. Do not allow small children or other family members to disturb the pup when he is eating; dogs like to enjoy their meals just like you do!

emerges and he begins to investigate the world around him. It is at this time when you may notice that the untrained dog begins to wander away from you and even ignore your commands to stay close. When this behavior becomes a problem, the owner has two choices: get rid of the dog or train him. It is strongly urged that you choose the latter option.

There are usually obedience classes within a reasonable distance from your home, but you also can do a lot to train your dog yourself. Sometimes there are classes available but the tuition is too costly. Whatever the circumstances, the solution to training your dog without formal obedience lessons lies within the pages of this book

This chapter is devoted to

helping you train your Dachshund at home. If the recommended procedures are followed faithfully, you may expect positive results that will prove rewarding both to you and your dog.

Whether your new charge is a puppy or a mature adult, the methods of teaching and the techniques we use in training basic behaviors are the same. After all, no dog, whether puppy or adult, likes harsh or inhumane methods. All creatures, however, respond favorably to gentle motivational methods and sincere praise and encouragement. Now let us get started.

HOUSEBREAKING

You can train a puppy to relieve himself wherever you choose, but this must be somewhere suitable. You should bear in mind from the outset that when your puppy is old enough to go out in public places, any canine deposits must be removed at once. You will always have to carry with you a small plastic bag or "poop-scoop."

Outdoor training includes such surfaces as grass, soil and cement. Indoor training usually means training your dog to newspaper.

When deciding on the surface and location that you

will want your Dachshund to use, be sure it is going to be permanent. Training your dog to grass and then changing your mind two months later is extremely difficult for both dog and owner.

Next, choose the command you will use each and every time you want your puppy to void. "Let's go," "Hurry up" and "Potty" are examples of commands commonly used by dog owners.

Get in the habit of giving

OBEDIENCE CLASSES

A basic obedience beginner's class usually lasts for six to eight weeks. Dog and owner attend an hour-long lesson once a week and practice for a few minutes, several times a day, each day at home, to reinforce the exercises learned each week in class. If done properly, the whole procedure will result in a well-mannered dog and an owner who delights in living with a pet that is eager to please and enjoys doing things with his owner.

Dachshunds can be attentive and willing students, provided the owner approaches training seriously and makes sessions positive and fun.

human babies, puppies need to relieve themselves frequently. Take your puppy out often—every hour for an eight-week-old, for example—and always immediately after sleeping and eating. The older the puppy, the less often he will need to relieve himself. Finally, as a mature healthy adult, he will require only three to five relief trips per day.

HOUSING

Since the types of housing and control you provide for your puppy have a direct relationship on the success of housebreaking, we consider the various aspects of both before we begin training.

Taking a new puppy home and turning him loose in your

Don't overdo the treats when you are house-training your Dachshund. Avoid fatty treats like cheese and hotdogs.

the puppy your chosen relief command before you take him out. That way, when he becomes an adult, you will be able to determine if he wants to go out when you ask him. A confirmation will be signs of interest, such as wagging his tail, watching you intently, going to the door, etc.

PUPPY'S NEEDS

Puppy needs to relieve himself after play periods, after each meal, after he has been sleeping and any time he indicates that he is looking for a place to urinate or defecate.

The urinary and intestinal tract muscles of very young puppies are not fully developed. Therefore, like

PAPER CAPER

Never line your pup's sleeping area with newspaper. Puppy litters are usually raised on newspaper and, once in your home, the puppy will immediately associate newspaper with voiding. Never put newspaper on any floor while house-breaking, as this will only confuse the puppy. If you are paper-training him, use paper in his designated relief area only. Finally, restrict water intake after evening meals. Offer a few licks at a time—never let a young puppy gulp water after meals. Once housebroken, the pup can have free access to water.

house can be compared to turning a child loose in a sports arena and telling the child that the place is all his! The sheer enormity of the place would be too much for him to handle.

Instead, offer the puppy clearly defined areas where he can play, sleep, eat and live. A room of the house where the family gathers is the most obvious choice. Puppies are social animals and need to feel a part of the pack right from the start. Hearing your voice, watching you while you are doing things and smelling you nearby are all positive reinforcers that he is now a member of your pack. Usually a family room, the kitchen or a nearby adjoining breakfast area is ideal for providing safety and security for both puppy and owner.

Within that room, there should be a smaller area that the puppy can call his own. An alcove, a wire or fiberglass dog crate or a fenced (not boarded!) corner from which he can view the activities of his new family will be fine. The size of the area or crate is the key factor here. The area must be large enough for the puppy to lie down and stretch out his super-long little body, yet small enough so that he cannot relieve himself at one end and sleep at the other

THINK BEFORE YOU BARK!

Dogs are sensitive to their masters' moods and emotions. Use your voice wisely when communicating with your

dog. Never raise your voice at your dog unless you are angry and trying to correct him. "Barking" at your dog can become as meaningless as "dogspeak" is to you.

without coming into contact with his droppings before he is fully trained to relieve himself outside.

Dogs are, by nature, clean animals and will not remain close to their relief areas unless forced to do so. In those cases, they then become dirty dogs and usually remain that way for life.

The designated area should be lined with clean bedding

CANINE DEVELOPMENT SCHEDULE

It is important to understand how and at what age a puppy develops into adulthood. If you are a puppy owner, consult the following Canine Development Schedule to determine the stage of development your puppy is currently experiencing. This knowledge will help you as you work with the puppy in the weeks and months ahead.

Period	Age	Characteristics
FIRST TO THIRD	BIRTH TO SEVEN WEEKS	Puppy needs food, sleep and warmth, and responds to simple and gentle touching. Needs mother for security and disciplining. Needs littermates for learning and interacting with other dogs. Pup learns to function within a pack and learns pack order of dominance. Begin socializing with adults and children for short periods. Begins to become aware of its environment.
FOURTH	EIGHT TO TWELVE WEEKS	Brain is fully developed. Needs socializing with outside world. Remove from mother and littermates. Needs to change from canine pack to human pack. Human dominance necessary. Fear period occurs between 8 and 16 weeks. Avoid fright and pain.
FIFTH	THIRTEEN TO SIXTEEN WEEKS	Training and formal obedience should begin. Less association with other dogs, more with people, places, situations. Period will pass easily if you remember this is pup's change-to-adolescence time. Be firm and fair. Flight instinct prominent. Permissiveness and over-disciplining can do permanent damage. Praise for good behavior.
JUVENILE	FOUR TO EIGHT MONTHS	Another fear period about 7 to 8 months of age. It passes quickly, but be cautious of fright and pain. Sexual maturity reached. Dominant traits established. Dog should understand sit, down, come and stay by now.

NOTE: THESE ARE APPROXIMATE TIME FRAMES. ALLOW FOR INDIVIDUAL DIFFERENCES IN PUPPIES.

and a toy. Water must always be available, in a non-spill container, once the dog is housebroken reliably.

CONTROL

By control, we mean helping the puppy to create a lifestyle pattern that will be compatible to that of his human pack *(you!)*. Just as we guide little children to learn our way of life, we must show the puppy when it is time to play, eat, sleep, exercise and even entertain himself.

Your puppy should always sleep in his crate. He should also learn that, during times of household confusion and excessive human activity such as at breakfast when family members are preparing for the day, he can play by himself in relative safety and comfort in his designated area. Each time

you leave the puppy alone, he should understand exactly where he is to stay. Puppies are chewers. They cannot tell the difference between lamp cords, television wires, shoes, table legs, etc. Chewing into a television wire, for example, can be fatal to the puppy, while a shorted wire can start a

Dachshunds enjoy all the comforts of home.

HOW MANY TIMES A DAY?

AGE	RELIEF TRIPS
To 14 weeks	10
14–22 weeks	8
22–32 weeks	6
Adulthood	4
(dog stops growing)	

These are estimates, of course, but they are a guide to the minimum opportunities a dog should have each day to relieve itself.

93

FEAR AGGRESSION

Pups who are subjected to physical abuse during training commonly end up with behavioral problems as adults. One common result of abuse is fear aggression, in which a dog will lash out, bare his teeth, snarl and finally bite someone by whom he feels threatened. For example, your daughter may be playing with the dog one afternoon. As they play hide-and-seek, she backs the dog into a corner and, as she attempts to tease him playfully, he bites her hand. Examine the cause of this behavior. Did your daughter ever hit the dog? Did someone who resembles your daughter hit or scream at the dog?

Fortunately, fear aggression is relatively easy to correct. Have your daughter engage in only positive activities with the dog, such as feeding, petting and walking. She should not give any corrections or negative feedback. If the dog still growls or cowers away from her, allow someone else to accompany them. After approximately one week, the dog should feel that he can rely on her for many positive things, and he will also be prevented from reacting fearfully towards anyone who might resemble her.

fire in the house.

If the puppy chews on the arm of the chair when he is alone, you will probably discipline him angrily when you get home. Thus, he makes the association that your coming home means he is going to be punished. (He will not remember chewing the chair and is incapable of making the association of the discipline with his naughty deed.)

Other times of excitement, such as family parties, etc., can be fun for the puppy, providing that he can view the activities from the security of his designated area. He is not underfoot and he is not being fed all sorts of tidbits that will probably cause him stomach distress, yet he still feels a part of the fun.

SCHEDULE

A puppy should be taken to his relief area each time he is released from his designated area, after meals, after play sessions and when he first awakens in the morning (at age eight weeks, this can mean 5 a.m.!). The puppy will indicate that he's ready "to go" by circling or sniffing busily— do not misinterpret these signs. For a puppy less than ten weeks of age, a routine of taking him out every hour is necessary. As the puppy grows, he will be able to wait for longer periods of time.

Keep trips to his relief area short. Stay no more than five or six minutes and then return to the house. If he goes during that time, praise him lavishly and take him indoors immediately. If he does not, but he has an accident when you go back indoors, pick him up immediately, say "No! No!" and return to his relief area. Wait a few minutes, then return to the house again. Never hit a puppy or rub his face in urine or excrement when he has had an accident!

Once indoors, put the puppy in his crate until you have had time to clean up his accident. Then release him to the family area and watch him more closely than before. Chances are, his accident was a result of your not picking up his signal or waiting too long before offering him the opportunity to relieve himself. Never hold a grudge against the puppy for accidents.

Let the puppy learn that going outdoors means it is time to relieve himself, not to play. Once trained, he will be able to play indoors and out and still differentiate between the times for play versus the times for relief.

Help him develop regular hours for naps, being alone, playing by himself and just resting, all in his crate. Encourage him to entertain himself while you are busy with your activities. Let him learn that having you near is comforting, but it is not your main purpose in life to provide him with undivided attention.

Each time you put a puppy in his own area, use the same command, whatever suits best. Soon he will run to his crate or special area when he hears you say those words.

Crate training provides safety for you, the puppy and

HOUSEBREAKING TIP

A consistent routine is the best way to housebreak a puppy. Always take your dog to the same location, always use the same command and always have the dog on leash when he is in his relief area, unless a fenced-in yard is available.

By following the Success Method, your puppy will be completely housebroken by the time his muscle and brain development reach maturity. Keep in mind that small breeds usually mature faster than large breeds, but all puppies should be trained by six months of age.

the home. It also provides the puppy with a feeling of security, and that helps the puppy achieve self-confidence and clean habits.

Remember that one of the primary ingredients in housebreaking your puppy is control. Regardless of your lifestyle, there will always be occasions when you will need to have a place where your dog can stay and be happy and safe. Crate training is the answer for now and in the future.

In conclusion, a few key

THE SUCCESS METHOD

Success that comes by luck is usually short-lived. Success that comes by well-thought-out proven methods is often more easily achieved and permanent. This is the Success Method. It is designed to give you, the puppy owner, a simple yet proven way to help your puppy develop clean living habits and a feeling of security in his new environment.

6 Steps to Successful Crate Training

1 Tell the puppy "Crate time!" and place him in the crate with a small treat (a piece of cheese or half of a biscuit). Let him stay in the crate for five minutes while you are in the same room. Then release him and praise lavishly. Never release him when he is fussing. Wait until he is quiet before you let him out.

2 Repeat Step 1 several times a day.

3 The next day, place the puppy in the crate as before. Let him stay there for ten minutes. Do this several times.

4 Continue building time in five-minute increments until the puppy stays in his crate for 30 minutes with you in the room. Always take him to his relief area after prolonged periods in his crate.

5 Now go back to Step 1 and let the puppy stay in his crate for five minutes, this time while you are out of the room.

6 Once again, build crate time in five-minute increments with you out of the room. When the puppy will stay willingly in his crate (he may even fall asleep!) for 30 minutes with you out of the room, he will be ready to stay in it for several hours at a time.

elements are really all you need for a successful housebreaking method—consistency, frequency, praise, control and supervision. By following these procedures with a normal, healthy puppy, you and the puppy will soon be past the stage of "accidents" and ready to move on to a full and rewarding life together.

ROLES OF DISCIPLINE, REWARD AND PUNISHMENT

Discipline, training one to act in accordance with rules, brings order to life. It is as simple as that. Without discipline, particularly in a group society, chaos reigns supreme and the group will eventually perish. Humans and canines are social animals and need some form of discipline

Always clean up after your dog, whether you're in a public place or your own yard.

in order to function effectively. They must procure food, protect their home base and their young and reproduce to keep the species going.

If there were no discipline in the lives of social animals, they would eventually die from starvation and/or predation by other stronger animals.

In the case of domestic canines, dogs need discipline in their lives in order to understand how their pack (you and other family members) functions and how they must act in order to survive.

A large humane society in a highly populated area recently surveyed dog owners regarding their satisfaction with their relationships with their dogs. People who had trained their dogs were 75% more satisfied with their pets than those who had never trained their dogs.

Dr. Edward Thorndike, a psychologist, established *Thorndike's Theory of Learning*, which states that a

THE CLEAN LIFE

By providing sleeping and resting quarters that fit the dog, and offering frequent opportunities to relieve himself outside his quarters, the puppy quickly learns that the outdoors (or the newspaper if you are training him to paper) is the place to go when he needs to urinate or defecate. It also reinforces his innate desire to keep his sleeping quarters clean. This, in turn, helps develop the muscle control that will eventually produce a dog with clean living habits.

CONSISTENCY PAYS OFF

Dogs need consistency in their feeding schedule, exercise and potty breaks, and in the verbal commands you use. If you use "Stay" on Monday and "Stay here,

please" on Tuesday, you will confuse your dog. Don't demand perfect behavior during training sessions and then let him have the run of the house the rest of the day. Above all, lavish praise on your pet consistently every time he does something right. Positive reinforcement is the key to success. The more he feels he is pleasing you, the more willing he will be to learn.

behavior that results in a pleasant event tends to be repeated. A behavior that results in an unpleasant event tends not to be repeated. It is this theory on which training methods are based today. For example, if you manipulate a dog to perform a specific behavior and reward him for doing it, he is likely to do it again because he enjoyed the end result.

Occasionally, punishment, a penalty inflicted for an offense, is necessary. The best type of punishment often comes from an outside source. For example, a child is told not to touch the stove because he may get burned. He disobeys and touches the stove. In doing so, he receives a burn. From that time on, he respects the heat of the stove and avoids contact with it. Therefore, a behavior that results in an unpleasant event tends not to be repeated.

A good example of a dog's learning the hard way is the dog who chases the house cat. He is told many times to leave the cat alone, yet he persists in teasing the cat. Then, one day he begins chasing the cat but the cat turns and swipes a claw across the dog's face, leaving him with a painful gash on his nose. The final result is that the dog stops chasing the cat.

During training sessions, you must be able to recognize signs of stress in your dog such as:

- tucking his tail between his legs
- lowering his head
- shivering or trembling
- standing completely still or running away
- panting and/or salivating
- avoiding eye contact
- flattening his ears back
- urinating submissively
- rolling over and lifting a leg
- grinning or baring teeth
- aggression when restrained

If your four-legged student displays these signs, he may just be nervous or intimidated. The training session may have been too lengthy, with not enough praise and affirmation. Stop for the day and try again tomorrow.

TRAINING EQUIPMENT

COLLAR AND LEASH

For a Dachshund, the collar and leash that you use for training must be one with which you are easily able to work, not too heavy for the dog and perfectly safe.

TREATS

Have a bag of treats on hand; something nutritious and easy to swallow works best. Use a soft treat, a chunk of cheese or a piece of cooked chicken rather than a dry biscuit. By the time the dog has finished chewing a dry treat, he will forget why he is being rewarded in the first place! Using food rewards will not teach a dog to beg at the table—the only way to teach a dog to beg at the table is to give him food from the table. In training, rewarding the dog with a food treat will help him associate praise and the treats with learning new behaviors that obviously please his owner.

TRAINING BEGINS: ASK THE DOG A QUESTION

In order to teach your dog anything, you must first get his attention. After all, he cannot learn anything if he is looking away from you with his mind on something else.

To get his attention, ask him, "School?" and immediately walk over to him and give him a treat as you tell him "Good dog." Wait a minute or two and repeat the routine, this time with a treat in your hand as you approach within a foot of the dog. Do not go directly to him, but stop about a foot short of him and hold out the treat as you ask, "School?" He will see you approaching with a treat in your hand and most likely begin walking toward you. As you meet, give him the treat and praise again.

99

PLAN TO PLAY

The puppy should also have regular play and exercise sessions when he is with you or a family member. Exercise for a very young puppy can consist of a short

walk around the house or yard. Playing can include fetching games with a large ball or a special chew toy. (All puppies teethe and need soft things upon which to chew.) Remember to restrict play periods to indoors within his living area (the family room, for example) until he is completely house-trained.

The third time, ask the question, have a treat in your hand and walk only a short distance toward the dog so that he must walk almost all the way to you. As he reaches you, give him the treat and praise again.

By this time, the dog will probably be getting the idea that if he pays attention to you, especially when you ask that question, it will pay off in treats and enjoyable activities for him. In other words, he learns that "school" means doing enjoyable things with you that result in treats and positive attention for him.

Remember that the dog does not understand your verbal language; he only recognizes sounds. Your question translates to a series of sounds for him, and those sounds become the signal to go to you and pay attention; if he does, he will get to interact with you plus receive treats and praise.

THE BASIC COMMANDS

TEACHING SIT

Now that you have the dog's attention, attach his leash and hold it in your left hand and a food treat in your right. Place your food hand at the dog's nose and let him lick the treat but not take it from you. Say "Sit" and slowly raise your food hand from in front of the dog's nose high up over his head so that he is looking at the ceiling. As he bends his head upward, he should have to bend his knees to maintain his balance. As he bends his knees, he will assume a sit position. At that point, release the food treat and praise lavishly with comments such as "Good dog! Good sit!," etc. Depending on your Dachshund, you may have to apply gentle pressure to his rear to encourage him to sit. Remember always to praise enthusiastically, because dogs relish verbal praise from their owners.

You will not use food forever in getting the dog to obey your commands. Food is only used to teach new behaviors, and once the dog knows what you want when you give a specific command, you will wean him off the food treats but still maintain the verbal praise. After all, you will always have your voice with you, and there will be many times when you have no food rewards but expect the dog to obey.

TEACHING DOWN

Teaching the down exercise is easy when you understand how the dog perceives the down position, and it is very difficult when you do not. Dogs

LANGUAGE BARRIER

Dogs do not understand our language. They can be trained to react to a certain sound, at a certain volume. If you say "No, Oliver" in a very soft, pleasant

voice, it will not have the same meaning as "No, Oliver!" when you shout it as loud as you can. You should never use the dog's name during a reprimand, just the command "NO!"

101

THE GOLDEN RULE

The golden rule of dog training is simple. For each "question" (command), there is only one correct answer (reaction). One

command = one reaction. Keep practicing the command until the dog reacts correctly without hesitating. Be repetitive but not monotonous. Dogs get bored just as people do; a bored dog's attention will not be focused on the lesson.

Have the dog sit close alongside your left leg, facing in the same direction as you are. Hold the leash in your left hand and a food treat in your right. Now place your left hand lightly on the top of the dog's shoulders where they meet above the spinal cord. Do not push down on the dog's shoulders; simply rest your left hand there so you can guide the dog to lie down close to your left leg rather than to swing away from your side when he drops.

Now place the food hand at the dog's nose, say "Down" very softly (almost a whisper) and slowly lower the food hand to the dog's front feet. When the food hand reaches the floor, begin moving it forward along the floor in front

Your Dachshund requires a light collar and leash that should fit snugly, but not tightly.

perceive the down position as a submissive one; therefore, teaching the down exercise using a forceful method can sometimes make the dog develop such a fear of the down that he either runs away when you say "Down" or he attempts to snap at the person who tries to force him down. Since Dachshunds are so low to the ground, teaching the down is hopefully easier than with a longer-legged, equally strong-willed dog.

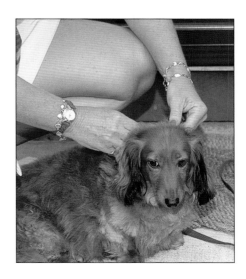

of the dog. Keep talking softly to the dog, saying things like, "Do you want this treat? You can do this, good dog." Your reassuring tone of voice will help calm the dog as he tries to follow the food hand in order to get the treat.

When the dog's elbows touch the floor, release the food and praise softly. Try to get the dog to maintain that down position for several seconds

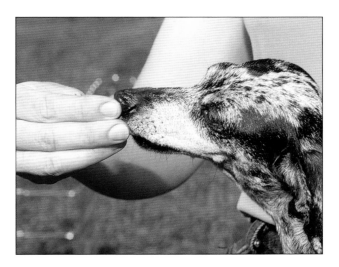

TAKE THE LEAD

Do not carry your dog to his relief area. Lead him there on a leash or, better yet, encourage him to follow

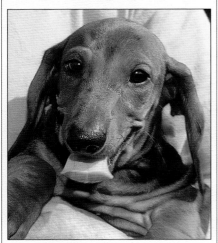

you to the spot. If you start carrying him to his spot, you might end up doing this routine forever and your dog will have the satisfaction of having trained you.

before you let him sit up again. The goal here is to get the dog to settle down and not feel threatened in the down position.

Treats make training easier, but breaking the treat habit can be a task in itself.

TEACHING STAY

It is easy to teach the dog to stay in either a sit or a down position. Again, we use food and praise during the teaching process as we help the dog to understand exactly what it is that we are expecting him to do.

To teach the sit/stay, start with the dog sitting on your left side as before and hold the leash in your left hand. Have a food treat in your right hand and place your food hand at the dog's nose. Say "Stay" and step out on your right foot to stand directly in front of the dog, toe to toe, as he licks and nibbles

Dachshund

Puppies that are destined for the show ring should be trained to stand from an early age. A squeaky toy is useful to get and hold the attention of the show-ring student.

the treat. Be sure to keep his head facing upward to maintain the sit position. Count to five and then swing around to stand next to the dog again with him on your left. As soon as you get back to the original position, release the food and praise lavishly.

To teach the down/stay, do the down as previously described. As soon as the dog lies down, say "Stay" and step out on your right foot just as you did in the sit/stay. Count to five and then return to stand beside the dog with him on your left side. Release the treat and praise as always.

Within a week or ten days, you can begin to add a bit of distance between you and your dog when you leave him. When you do, use your left hand open with the palm facing the dog as a stay signal, much the same as the hand signal a police officer uses to stop traffic at an intersection. Hold the food treat in your right hand as before, but this time the food should not be touching the dog's nose. He will watch the food hand and quickly learn that he is going to get that treat as soon as you return to his side.

When you can stand 3 feet away from your dog for 30 seconds, you can then begin building time and distance in

"COME"... BACK

Never call your dog to come to you for a correction or scold him when he reaches you. That is the quickest way to turn a "Come" command into "Go away fast!" Dogs think only in the present tense, and your dog will connect the punishment with coming to you, not with the misbehavior of a few moments earlier.

both stays. Eventually, the dog can be expected to remain in the stay position for prolonged periods of time until you return to him or call him to you. Always praise lavishly when he stays.

PRACTICE MAKES PERFECT!

- Have training lessons with your dog every day in several short segments—three to five times a day for a few minutes at a time is ideal.

- Do not have long practice sessions. The dog will become easily bored.
- Never practice when you are tired, ill, worried or in an otherwise negative mood. This will transmit to the dog and may have an adverse effect on its performance.

  Think fun, short and *positive!* End each session on a high note, rather than a failed exercise, and make sure to give a lot of praise. Enjoy the training and help your dog enjoy it, too.

TEACHING COME

If you make teaching "come" an enjoyable experience, you should never have a "student" that does not love the game or that fails to come when called. The secret, it seems, is never to teach the word "come."

At times when an owner most wants his dog to come when called, the owner is likely upset or anxious and he allows these feelings to come through in the tone of his voice when he calls his dog. Hearing that desperation in his owner's voice, the dog fears the results of going to him and therefore either disobeys outright or runs in the opposite direction. The secret, therefore, is to teach the dog a game and, when you want him to come to you, simply play the game. It is practically a no-fail solution!

To begin, have several

members of your family take a few food treats and each go into a different room in the house. Take turns calling the dog, and each person should celebrate the dog's finding him with a treat and lots of happy praise. When a person calls the dog, he is actually inviting the dog to find him and get a treat as a reward for "winning."

A few turns of the "Where are you?" game and the dog will understand that everyone is playing the game and that each person has a big celebration awaiting the dog's success at locating him or her. Once he learns to love the game, simply calling out "Where are you?" will bring him running from wherever he is when he hears that all-important question.

The come command is recognized as one of the most important things to teach a dog, but there are trainers who work with thousands of dogs and never teach the actual word "come." Yet these dogs will race to respond to a person who uses the dog's name followed by "Where are you?" For example, a woman has a 12-year-old companion dog who went blind, but who never fails to locate her owner when asked, "Where are you?"

Children, in particular, love to play this game with their dogs. Children can hide in smaller places like a shower or bathtub, behind a bed or under a table. The dog needs to work a little bit harder to find these hiding places but, when he does, he loves to celebrate with a treat and a tussle with a favorite youngster.

TEACHING HEEL
Heeling means that the dog walks beside the owner without pulling. It takes time and patience on the owner's

FETCH!

Play fetch games with your puppy in an enclosed area where he can retrieve his toy and bring it back to you. Always use a toy or object designated just for this purpose. Never use a shoe, sock or other item that he may later confuse with those in your closet or underneath your chair.

Dachshunds make attentive and bright students, or at least they photograph that way!

the loop end of the leash to your right hand but keep your left hand short on the leash so that it keeps the dog in close next to you.

Say "Heel" and step forward on your left foot. Keep the dog close to you and take

COMMAND STANCE

Stand up straight and authoritatively when giving your dog commands. Do not issue commands when lying on the floor or lying on your back on the sofa. If you are on your hands and knees when you give a command, your dog will think you are ready to play.

part to succeed at teaching the dog that he (the owner) will not proceed unless the dog is walking calmly beside him. Pulling out ahead on the leash is definitely not acceptable.

Begin by holding the leash in your left hand as the dog sits beside your left leg. Move three steps. Stop and have the dog sit next to you in what we now call the heel position. Praise verbally, but do not touch the dog. Hesitate a moment and begin again with "Heel," taking three steps and stopping, at which point the dog is told to sit again.

Your goal here is to have the dog walk those three steps without pulling on the leash. Once he will walk calmly beside you for three steps without pulling, increase the number of steps you take to five. When he will walk politely beside you while you take five steps, you can increase the length of your walk to ten steps. Keep increasing the length of your stroll until the dog will walk quietly beside you without pulling as long as you want him to heel. When you stop heeling, indicate to the dog that the exercise is over by verbally praising as you pet him and say "OK, good dog." The "OK" is used as a release word, meaning that the exercise is finished and the dog is free to relax.

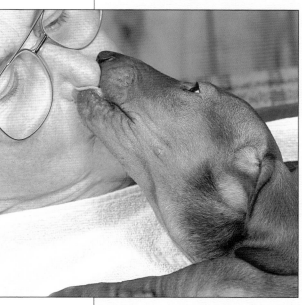

SAFETY FIRST

While it may seem that the most important things to your dog are eating, sleeping and chewing the upholstery on your furniture, his first concern is actually safety. The domesticated dogs we keep as companions have the same pack instinct as their ancestors who ran free thousands of years ago. Because of this pack instinct, your dog wants to know that he and his pack are not in danger of being harmed, and that his pack has a strong, capable leader. You must establish yourself as the leader early on in your relationship. That way your dog will trust that you will take care of him and the pack, and he will accept your commands without question.

TRAINING TIP

If you begin teaching the heel by taking long walks and letting the dog pull you along, he misinterprets this action as an acceptable form of taking a walk. When you pull back on the leash to counteract his pulling, he reads that tug as a signal to pull even harder!

If you are dealing with a dog who insists on pulling you around, simply "put on your brakes" and stand your ground until the dog realizes that the two of you are not going anywhere until he is beside you and moving at your pace, not his. It may take some time just standing there to

convince the dog that you are the leader and you will be the one to decide on the direction and speed of your travel.

Each time the dog looks up at you or slows down to give a slack leash between the two of you, quietly praise him and say, "Good heel. Good dog." Eventually, the dog will begin to respond and within a few days he will be walking politely beside you without pulling on the leash. At first, the training sessions should be kept short and very positive; soon the dog will be able to walk nicely with you for increasingly longer distances. Remember also to give the dog free time and the opportunity to run and play when you have finished heel practice.

WEANING OFF FOOD IN TRAINING
Food is used in training new behaviors. Once the dog understands what behavior goes with a specific command, it is time to start weaning him off the food treats. At first, give a treat after each exercise. Then, start to give a treat only after every other exercise. Mix up the times when you offer a food reward and the times when you only offer praise so that the dog will never know when he is going to receive both food and praise and

when he is going to receive only praise. This is called a variable ratio reward system and it proves successful because there is always the chance that the owner will produce a treat, so the dog never stops trying for that reward. No matter what, *always* give verbal praise.

OBEDIENCE CLASSES

It is a good idea to enroll in an obedience class if one is available in your area. If yours is a show dog, ringcraft classes would be more appropriate. Many areas have dog clubs that offer basic obedience training as well as preparatory classes for obedience competition. There are also local dog trainers who offer similar classes.

At obedience trials, dogs can earn titles at various levels of competition. The beginning levels of competition include basic behaviors such as sit, down, heel, etc. The more advanced levels of competition include retrieving, scent discrimination and signal work. The advanced levels require a dog and owner to put a lot of time and effort into their training, and the titles that can be earned at these levels of competition are very prestigious.

OTHER ACTIVITIES FOR LIFE

Whether a dog is trained in the structured environment of a class or alone with his owner at home, there are many activities that can bring fun and rewards to both owner and dog once they have mastered basic control.

Teaching the dog to help out around the home, in the

LEAD THE WAY

If you are walking your dog and he suddenly stops and looks straight into your eyes, ignore him. Pull the leash and continue to walk, leading him in the direction you want to walk.

HOW TO WEAN THE "TREAT HOG"

If you have trained your dog by rewarding him with a treat each time he performs a command, he may soon decide that without the treat, he won't sit, stay or come. The best way to fix

this problem is to start asking your dog to do certain commands twice before being rewarded. Slowly increase the number of commands given and then vary the number: three sits and a treat one day, five sits for a biscuit the next day, etc. Your dog will soon realize that there is no set number of sits before he gets his reward and he'll likely do it the first time you ask in the hope of being rewarded sooner rather than later.

yard or on the farm provides great satisfaction to both dog and owner. In addition, the dog's help makes life a little easier for his owner and raises his stature as a valued companion to his family. It helps give the dog a purpose by occupying his mind and providing an outlet for his energy.

If you are interested in participating in organized competition with your Dachshund, there are activities other than obedience in which you and your dog can become involved. Earthdog tests are ideal for the Dachshund, giving the dog the chance to hone his excavating techniques.

Likewise, agility is a sport in which dogs run through obstacle courses that include various tunnels and other exercises to test the dogs' speed and coordination. The owners run beside their dogs to give commands and to guide them through the obstacles. Although competitive, the focus is on fun—it's fun to do, fun to watch and great exercise.

Top and bottom left: Dachshunds compete in earthdog trials, competing against the terrier breeds. Of course, the Dachshund was built for digging and naturally excels in these trials.

HELPING PAWS

Your dog may not be the next Lassie, but every pet has the potential to do some tricks well. Identify his natural talents and hone them. Is your dog always happy and upbeat? Teach him to wag his tail or give you his paw on command. Dogs also can be trained to do household chores, such as retrieving the morning paper.

113

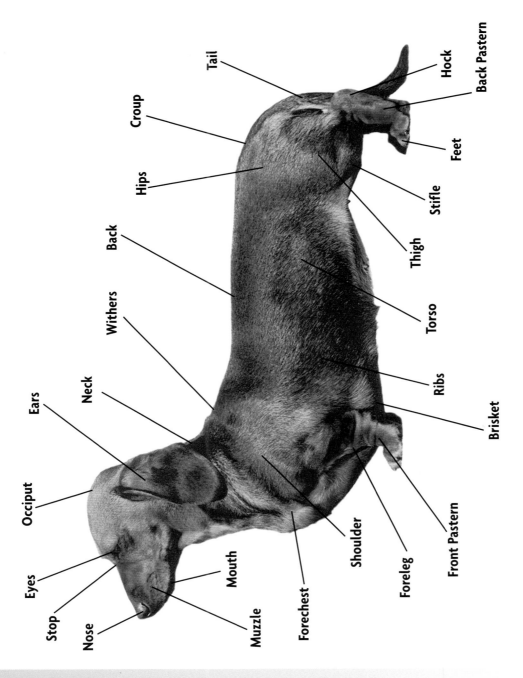

Tail

Croup

Hips

Back

Withers

Neck

Ears

Occiput

Eyes

Stop

Nose

Muzzle

Mouth

Forechest

Shoulder

Foreleg

Front Pastern

Brisket

Ribs

Torso

Thigh

Stifle

Feet

Hock

Back Pastern

Physical Structure of the Dachshund

Dogs suffer from many of the same physical illnesses as people. They might even share many of the same psychological problems. Since people usually know more about human diseases than canine maladies, many of the terms used in this chapter will be familiar but not necessarily those used by veterinarians. For example, we will use the familiar term *x-ray* instead of *radiograph*. We will also use the familiar term *symptoms*, even though dogs don't have symptoms, which are verbal descriptions of something the patient feels or observes himself that he regards as abnormal. Dogs have *clinical signs* since they cannot speak, so we have to look for these clinical signs...but we still use the term *symptoms* in the book.

Medicine is a constantly changing art, with some scientific input as well. Things alter as we learn more and more about basic sciences such as genetics and biochemistry, and have use of more sophisticated imaging techniques like Computer Aided Tomography (CAT scans) or Magnetic Resonance Imaging (MRI scans). There is academic dispute about many canine maladies, so different veterinarians treat them in different ways, and some vets place a greater emphasis on surgical techniques than others.

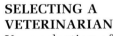

SELECTING A VETERINARIAN

Your selection of a veterinarian should be based on personal recommendation for their skills with dogs, and, if possible, especially Dachshunds. If the vet is based nearby, it will be helpful because you might have an emergency or need to make multiple visits for treatments.

You will require a local vet who will know your dog from puppyhood onward and who can monitor vaccination scheduling, diet and overall health.

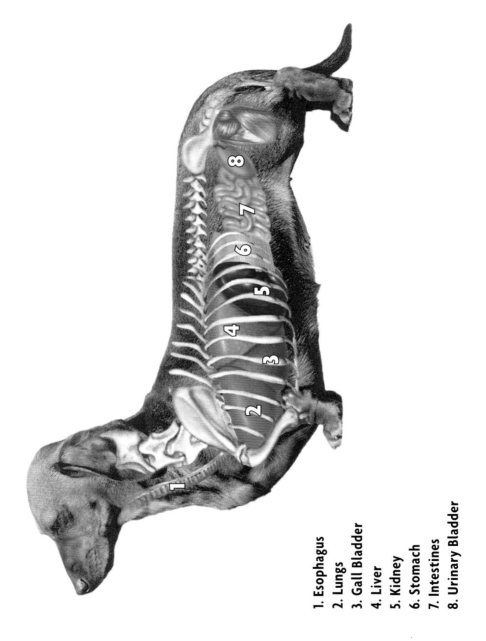

1. Esophagus
2. Lungs
3. Gall Bladder
4. Liver
5. Kidney
6. Stomach
7. Intestines
8. Urinary Bladder

Internal Organs of the Dachshund

All veterinarians are licensed and are capable of dealing with routine medical issues such as infections, injuries and the promotion of health (for example, by vaccination). If the problem affecting your dog is more complex, your veterinarian will refer your pet to someone with a more detailed knowledge of what is wrong. This will usually be a specialist who is a veterinary dermatologist, veterinary ophthalmologist, etc., whatever field you require.

Veterinary procedures are very costly and, as the treatments available improve, they are going to become more expensive. It is quite acceptable to discuss matters of cost with your vet; if there is more than one treatment option, cost may be a factor in deciding which route to take.

PREVENTATIVE MEDICINE
It is much easier, less costly and more effective to practice preventative medicine than to fight bouts of illness and disease. Properly

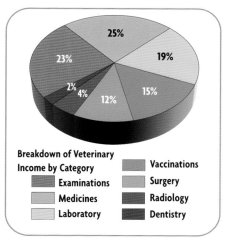

A typical vet's income, categorized according to services provided.

Breakdown of Veterinary Income by Category

- Examinations
- Medicines
- Laboratory
- Vaccinations
- Surgery
- Radiology
- Dentistry

25% | 19% | 23% | 2% | 4% | 12% | 15%

NEUTERING/SPAYING

Male dogs are castrated. The operation removes both testicles under general anesthesia. Recovery takes about one week. Females are spayed, in which the uterus and both of the ovaries are removed. This is major surgery, also under general anesthesia, and it usually takes a bitch two weeks to recover.

bred puppies of all breeds come from parents that were selected based upon their genetic disease profile. The puppies' mother should have been vaccinated, free of all internal and external parasites and properly nourished. For these reasons, a visit to the veterinarian who cared for the dam (mother) is recommended if at all possible. The dam passes disease resistance to her puppies, which should last from eight to ten weeks. Unfortunately, she can also pass on parasites and infection. This is why knowledge about her health is useful in learning more about the health of the puppies.

WEANING TO FIVE MONTHS OLD
Puppies should be weaned by the time they are two months old. A puppy that remains for at least eight weeks with its mother and

117

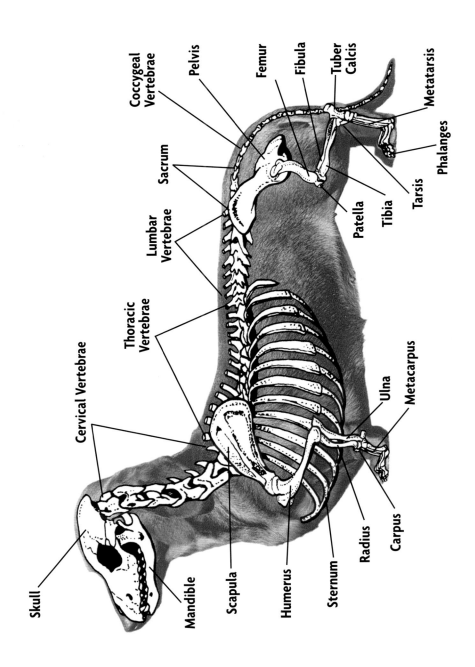

Coccygeal Vertebrae
Pelvis
Femur
Fibula
Tuber Calcis
Metatarsis
Phalanges
Sacrum
Tarsis
Tibia
Patella
Lumbar Vertebrae
Thoracic Vertebrae
Cervical Vertebrae
Metacarpus
Ulna
Carpus
Radius
Sternum
Humerus
Scapula
Mandible
Skull

Skeletal Structure of the Dachshund

littermates usually adapts better to other dogs and people later in its life.

Some new owners have their puppy examined by a veterinarian immediately, which is a good idea unless the puppy is overtired by a long journey. Vaccination programs usually begin when the puppy is very young.

The puppy will have its teeth examined and have its skeletal conformation and general health checked prior to certification by the veterinarian. Puppies in certain breeds have problems with their kneecaps, cataracts and other eye problems, heart murmurs and undescended testicles. They may also have personality problems and your veterinarian might have training in temperament evaluation.

VACCINATION SCHEDULING

Most vaccinations are given by injection and should only be given by a veterinarian. Both he and you should keep a record of the date of the injection, the identification of the vaccine and the amount given. Some vets give a first vaccination at eight weeks, but most dog breeders prefer the course not to commence until about ten weeks because of interaction with the antibodies produced by the mother. The vaccination scheduling is usually based on a 15-day cycle. You must take your vet's advice as to when

MORE THAN VACCINES

Vaccinations help prevent your new puppy from contracting diseases, but they do not cure them. Proper nutrition as well as parasite control keep your dog healthy and less susceptible to many dangerous diseases. Remember that your dog depends on you to ensure his well-being.

to vaccinate, as this may differ according to the vaccine used.

The usual vaccines contain immunizing doses of several different viruses such as distemper, parvovirus, parainfluenza and hepatitis. There are other vaccines available when the puppy is at risk. You should rely upon professional advice. This is especially true for the booster immunizations. Most vaccination programs require a booster when the puppy is a year old and once a year thereafter. In some cases, circumstances may require more frequent immunizations.

Canine cough, more formally known as tracheobronchitis, is immunized against with a vaccine that is sprayed into the dog's nostrils. Canine cough is usually included in routine vaccination, but it is often not as effective as the vaccines for other major diseases.

Your veterinarian will probably recommend that your

119

Normal hairs of a dog enlarged 200 times original size. The cuticle (outer covering) is clean and healthy. Unlike human hair that grows from the base, dog's hair also grows from the end, as shown in the inset.

puppy be fully vaccinated before you bring him outside. There are airborne diseases, parasite eggs in the grass and unexpected visits from other dogs that might be dangerous to your puppy's health. Other dogs are the most harmful reservoir of pathogenic organisms, as everything they have can be transmitted to your puppy.

FIVE MONTHS TO ONE YEAR OF AGE
Unless you intend to breed or show your dog, neutering the puppy at six months of age is recommended. Discuss this with your veterinarian. Neutering/ spaying has proven to be extremely beneficial to male and female puppies, respectively. Besides eliminating the possibility of pregnancy, it inhibits (but does

not prevent) breast cancer in bitches and prostate cancer in male dogs. Under no circumstances should a bitch be spayed prior to her first season.

Your veterinarian should provide your puppy with a thorough dental evaluation at six months of age, ascertaining whether all the permanent teeth have erupted properly. A home dental care regimen should be initiated at six months, including brushing weekly and providing good dental devices (such as nylon bones). Regular dental care promotes healthy teeth, fresh breath and a longer life.

DOGS OLDER THAN ONE YEAR
Continue to visit the veterinarian at least once a year. There is no such disease as "old age," but bodily functions do change with age. The eyes and ears are no longer as efficient. Liver, kidney and intestinal functions often decline. Proper dietary changes, recommended by your veterinarian, can make life more pleasant for your aging Dachshund and you.

SKIN PROBLEMS
Veterinarians are consulted by dog owners for skin problems more than for any other group of diseases or maladies. A dog's skin is as sensitive, if not more so, than human skin, and both suffer almost the same ailments (though

KNOW WHEN TO POSTPONE A VACCINATION

While the visit to the vet is costly, it is never advisable to update a vaccination when visiting with a sick or pregnant dog. Vaccinations should be avoided for all elderly dogs. If your dog is showing the signs of any illness or any medical condition, no matter how serious or mild, including skin irritations, do not vaccinate. Likewise, a lame dog should never be vaccinated; any dog undergoing surgery or on any immunosuppressant drugs should not be vaccinated until fully recovered.

HEALTH AND VACCINATION SCHEDULE

Age in Weeks:	6th	8th	10th	12th	14th	16th	20-24th	52nd
Worm Control	✔	✔	✔	✔	✔	✔	✔	
Neutering								✔
Heartworm		✔		✔		✔	✔	
Parvovirus	✔		✔		✔		✔	✔
Distemper		✔		✔		✔		✔
Hepatitis		✔		✔		✔		✔
Leptospirosis								✔
Parainfluenza	✔		✔		✔			✔
Dental Examination		✔					✔	✔
Complete Physical		✔					✔	✔
Coronavirus				✔			✔	✔
Canine Cough	✔							
Hip Dysplasia								✔
Rabies							✔	

Vaccinations are not instantly effective. It takes about two weeks for the dog's immune system to develop antibodies. Most vaccinations require annual booster shots. Your veterinarian should guide you in this regard.

the occurrence of acne in most breeds of dog is rare!). For this reason, veterinary dermatology has developed into a specialty practiced by many veterinarians.

Since many skin problems have visual symptoms that are almost identical, it requires the skill of an experienced veterinary dermatologist to identify and cure many of the more severe skin disorders. Pet shops sell many treatments for skin problems, but most of the treatments are directed at symptoms and not at the underlying problem(s). If your dog is suffering from a skin disorder, you should seek profes-sional assistance as quickly as possible. As with all diseases, the earlier a problem is identified and treated, the more likely that the cure will be successful.

HEREDITARY SKIN DISORDERS
Many skin disorders are inherited, and responsible Dachshund breeders are aware of these, as well as of those that derive from unknown causes. Sebaceous adenitis, a common skin problem in the Poodle, also affects the Dachshund, as does cutaneous asthenia, black-hair follicular dysplasia, body fold dermatitis, pinnal alopecia and pattern alopecia. Not all of these

are congenital diseases like sebaceous adenitis, but some hereditary links are suspected.

All inherited diseases must be diagnosed and treated by a veterinary specialist. There are active programs being undertaken by many veterinary pharmaceutical manufacturers to solve most, if not all, of the common skin problems in dogs.

PARASITE BITES

Many of us are allergic to insect bites. The bites itch, erupt and may even become infected. Dogs have the same reaction to fleas, ticks and/or mites. When an insect lands on you, you have the chance to whisk it away with your hand. Unfortunately, when a dog is bitten by a flea, tick or mite, it can only scratch it away or bite it. By the time the dog has been bitten, the parasite has done some of its damage. It may also have laid eggs, which will cause further problems in the near future. The itching from parasite bites is probably due to the saliva

DISEASE REFERENCE CHART

	What is it?	What causes it?	Symptoms
Leptospirosis	Severe disease that affects the internal organs; can be spread to people.	A bacterium, which is often carried by rodents, that enters through mucus membranes and spreads quickly throughout the body.	Range from fever, vomiting and loss of appetite in less severe cases to shock, irreversible kidney damage and possibly death in most severe cases.
Rabies	Potentially deadly virus that infects warm-blooded mammals.	Bite from a carrier of the virus, mainly wild animals.	1st stage: dog exhibits change in behavior, fear. 2nd stage: dog's behavior becomes more aggressive. 3rd stage: loss of coordination, trouble with bodily functions.
Parvovirus	Highly contagious virus, potentially deadly.	Ingestion of the virus, which is usually spread through the feces of infected dogs.	Most common: severe diarrhea. Also vomiting, fatigue, lack of appetite.
Canine cough	Contagious respiratory infection.	Combination of types of bacteria and virus. Most common: *Bordetella bronchiseptica* bacteria and parainfluenza virus.	Chronic cough.
Distemper	Disease primarily affecting respiratory and nervous system.	Virus that is related to the human measles virus.	Mild symptoms such as fever, lack of appetite and mucus secretion progress to evidence of brain damage, "hard pad."
Hepatitis	Virus primarily affecting the liver.	Canine adenovirus type I (CAV-1). Enters system when dog breathes in particles.	Lesser symptoms include listlessness, diarrhea, vomiting. More severe symptoms include "blue-eye" (clumps of virus in eye).
Coronavirus	Virus resulting in digestive problems.	Virus is spread through infected dog's feces.	Stomach upset evidenced by lack of appetite, vomiting, diarrhea.

Grass allergies and other airborne allergies are common ailments with Dachshunds as well as other breeds. Often the summer months are the worst for grass allergies, so wipe off your dog after he's been playing in the grass.

AUTO-IMMUNE ILLNESSES

An auto-immune illness is one in which the immune system overacts and does not recognize parts of the affected person; rather, the immune system starts to react as if these parts were foreign and need to be destroyed. An example is rheumatoid arthritis, which occurs when the body does not recognize the joints, thus leading to a very painful and damaging reaction in the joints. This has nothing to do with age, so can occur in children. The wear-and-tear arthritis of the older person or dog is called osteoarthritis.

injected into the site when the parasite sucks the dog's blood.

AIRBORNE ALLERGIES

Just as humans have hay fever from which they suffer during the pollinating season, many dogs suffer from the same allergies. When the pollen count is high, your dog might suffer but don't expect them to sneeze and have runny noses like humans. Dogs react to pollen allergies in the same way they react to flea—they scratch and bite themselves.

Dogs, like humans, can be tested for allergens. Discuss the testing with your veterinarian.

A SKUNKY PROBLEM

Have you noticed your dog dragging his backside along the floor? If so, it is likely that his anal sacs are impacted or possibly infected. The anal sacs are small pouches located on both sides of the anus under the skin and muscles. They are about the size and shape of a grape and contain a foul-smelling liquid. Their contents are usually emptied when the dog has a bowel movement but, if not emptied completely, they will impact, which will cause your dog much pain. Fortunately, your veterinarian can tend to this problem easily by draining the sacs for the dog. Be aware that your dog might also empty his anal sacs in cases of extreme fright.

First Aid at a Glance

Burns
Place the affected area under cool water; use ice if only a small area is burned.

Bee sting/Insect bites
Apply ice to relieve swelling; antihistamine dosed properly.

Animal bites
Clean any bleeding area; apply pressure until bleeding subsides; go to the vet.

Spider bites
Use cold compress and a pressurized pack to inhibit venom's spreading.

Antifreeze poisoning
Induce vomiting with hydrogen peroxide. Seek *immediate* veterinary help!

Fish hooks
Removal best handled by vet; hook must be cut in order to remove.

Snake bites
Pack ice around bite; contact vet quickly; identify snake for proper antivenin.

Car accident
Move dog from roadway with blanket; seek veterinary aid.

Shock
Calm the dog, keep him warm; seek immediate veterinary help.

Nosebleed
Apply cold compress to the nose; apply pressure to any visible abrasion.

Bleeding
Apply pressure above the area; treat wound by applying a cotton pack.

Heat stroke
Submerge dog in cold bath; cool down with fresh air and water; go to the vet.

Frostbite/Hypothermia
Warm the dog with a warm bath, electric blankets or hot water bottles.

Abrasions
Clean the wound and wash out thoroughly with fresh water; apply antiseptic.

 Remember: an injured dog may attempt to bite a helping hand from fear and confusion. Always muzzle the dog before trying to offer assistance.

Lupus is an auto-immune disease that affects dogs as well as people. It can take variable forms, affecting the kidneys, bones and the skin. It can be fatal, so is treated with steroids, which can themselves have very significant side effects. The steroids calm down the allergic reaction to the body's tissues, which helps the lupus, but also calms down the body's reaction to real foreign substances such as bacteria, and also thins the skin and bones.

FOOD PROBLEMS

Feeding your dog properly is very important. An incorrect diet could affect the dog's health, behavior and nervous system, possibly making a normal dog into an aggressive one. Its most visible effects are to the skin and coat, but internal organs are similarly affected.

FOOD ALLERGIES

Dogs are allergic to many foods that are best-sellers and highly recommended by breeders and veterinarians. Changing the brand of food that you buy may not eliminate the problem if the element to which the dog is allergic is contained in the new brand.

Recognizing a food allergy can be difficult. Humans often have rashes when they eat foods to which they are allergic, or have swelling of the lips or eyes. Dogs do not usually develop rashes, but react in the same way as they to an airborne or bite allergy—they itch, scratch and bite. While pollen allergies and parasite bites are usually seasonal, pollen allergies are year-round problems.

TREATING FOOD ALLERGY

Diagnosis of a food allergy is based on a two- to four-week dietary trial with a home-cooked diet fed to the exclusion of all other foods. The diet should consist of boiled rice or potato with a source of protein that the dog has never eaten before,

PET ADVANTAGES

If you do not intend to show or breed your new puppy, your vet and breeder will recommend that you spay your female or neuter your male. In the Dachshund, neutering can lead to weight gain, but if you feed and exercise your dog properly, this is easily avoided. Spaying or neutering can actually have many positive outcomes, such as:

- training becomes easier, as the dog focuses less on the urge to mate and more on you!
- females are protected from unplanned pregnancy as well as ovarian and uterine cancers.
- males are guarded from testicular tumors and have a reduced risk of developing prostate cancer.

Talk to your vet regarding the right age to spay/neuter and other aspects of the procedure.

such as fresh or frozen fish, lamb or even something as exotic as pheasant. Water has to be the only drink, and it is really important that no other foods are fed during this trial. If the dog's condition improves, you will need to try the original diet once again to see if the itching resumes. If it does, then this confirms the diagnosis that the dog is allergic to its original diet. The treatment is long-term feeding of something that does not distress the dog's skin, which may be in the form of one of the commercially available hypoallergenic diets or the home-made diet that you created for the allergy trial.

FOOD INTOLERANCE

Food intolerance is the inability of the dog to completely digest certain foods. This occurs because the dog does not have the chemicals necessary to digest some foodstuffs. These chemicals are called enzymes. All puppies have the enzymes necessary to digest canine milk, but some dogs do not have the enzymes to digest a very different form of milk that is commonly found in human households—milk from cows. In such dogs, drinking cows' milk results in loose bowels, stomach pains and the passage of gas.

Dogs often do not have the enzymes to digest soy or other beans. The treatment is to exclude the foodstuffs that upset your Dachshund's digestion.

DENTAL HEALTH

A dental examination is in order when the dog is between six months and one year of age so that any permanent teeth that have erupted incorrectly can be corrected. It is important to begin a brushing routine at home and stick to it every week. In time the dog will accept the procedure and not fuss every time you brush. Durable nylon and safe edible

chews should be a part of your Dachshund's arsenal for good health, good teeth and pleasant breath. The vast majority of dogs three to four years old and older has diseases of the gums from lack of dental attention. Using the various types of dental chews can be very effective in controlling dental plaque.

A male dog flea,
***Ctenocephalides
canis.***

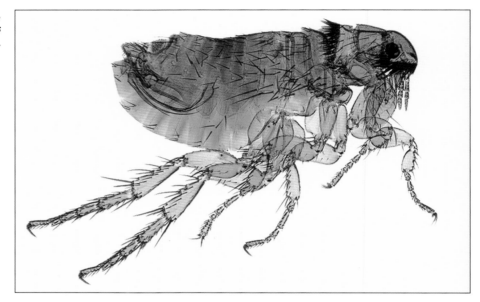

EXTERNAL PARASITES

FLEAS
Of all the problems to which dogs are prone, none is more well known and frustrating than fleas. Flea infestation is relatively simple to cure but difficult to prevent. Parasites that are harbored inside the body are a bit more difficult to eradicate but they are easier to control.

To control flea infestation, you have to understand the flea's life cycle. Fleas are often thought of as a summertime problem, but centrally heated homes have changed the patterns and fleas can be found at any time of the year. The most effective method of flea control is a two-stage approach: one stage to kill the adult fleas, and the other to control the development of pre-adult fleas. Unfortunately, no single active ingredient is effective against all stages of the life cycle.

FLEA KILLER CAUTION— "POISON"

Flea-killers are poisonous. You should not spray these toxic chemicals on areas of a dog's body that he licks, including his genitals and his face. Flea killers taken internally are a better answer, but check with your vet in case internal therapy is not advised for your dog.

LIFE CYCLE STAGES

During its life, a flea will pass through four life stages: egg, larva, pupa or nymph and adult. The adult stage is the most visible and irritating stage of the flea life cycle, and this is why the majority of flea-control products concentrate on this stage. The fact is that adult fleas account for only 1% of the total flea population, and the other 99% exist in pre-adult stages, i.e., eggs, larvae and nymphs. The pre-adult stages are barely visible to the naked eye.

THE LIFE CYCLE OF THE FLEA

Eggs are laid on the dog, usually in quantities of about 20 or 30, several times a day. The adult female flea must have a blood meal before each egg-laying session. When first laid, the eggs will cling to the dog's hair, as the eggs are still moist. However, they will quickly dry out and fall from the dog, especially if the dog moves around or scratches. Many eggs will fall off in the dog's favorite area or an area in which he spends a lot of time, such as his bed.

Once the eggs fall from the dog onto the carpet or furniture, they will hatch into larvae. This takes from one to ten days. Larvae are not particularly mobile and will usually travel only a few inches from where they hatch. However, they do have a tendency to move away from bright light and heavy

EN GARDE: CATCHING FLEAS OFF GUARD

Consider the following ways to arm yourself against fleas:
- Add a small amount of pennyroyal or eucalyptus oil to your dog's bath. These natural remedies repel fleas.
- Supplement your dog's food with fresh garlic (minced or grated) and a hearty amount of brewer's yeast, both of which ward off fleas.
- Use a flea comb on your dog daily. Submerge fleas in a cup of bleach to kill them quickly.
- Confine the dog to only a few rooms to limit the spread of fleas in the home.
- Vacuum daily . . . and get all of the crevices! Dispose of the bag every few days until the problem is under control.
- Wash your dog's bedding daily. Cover cushions where your dog sleeps with towels, and wash the towels often.

traffic—under furniture and behind doors are common places to find high quantities of flea larvae.

The flea larvae feed on dead organic matter, including adult flea feces, until they are ready to change into adult fleas. Fleas will usually remain as larvae for around seven days. After this period, the larvae will pupate into protective pupae. While inside the pupae, the larvae will undergo metamorphosis and change into adult fleas. This can take as little time as a few days, but the adult fleas can remain inside the pupae waiting to hatch for up to two years. The pupae are signaled to hatch by certain stimuli, such as physical pressure—the pupae's being stepped on, heat from an animal's lying on the pupae or increased carbon-dioxide levels and vibrations—indicating that a suitable host is available.

Once hatched, the adult flea must feed within a few days. Once the adult flea finds a host, it will not leave voluntarily. It only becomes dislodged by grooming or the host animal's scratching.

A scanning electron micrograph of a dog or cat flea, *Ctenocephalides*, magnified more than 100x. This image has been colorized for effect.

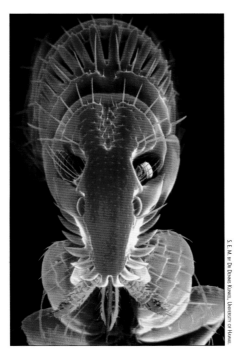

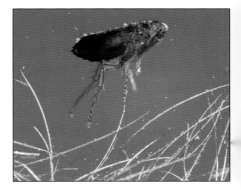

The adult flea will remain on the host for the duration of its life unless forcibly removed.

TREATING THE ENVIRONMENT AND THE DOG

Treating fleas should be a two-pronged attack. First, the environment needs to be treated; this includes carpets and furniture, especially the dog's bedding and areas underneath furniture. The environment should be treated with a household spray containing an Insect Growth Regulator (IGR) and an insecticide to kill the adult fleas. Most IGRs are effective against eggs and larvae; they actually mimic the fleas' own hormones and stop the eggs and larvae from developing into adult fleas. There are currently no treatments available to attack the pupa stage of the life cycle, so the adult insecticide is used to kill the newly hatched adult fleas before they find a host. Most IGRs are active for many months, while

S. E. M. BY DR DENNIS KUNKEL, UNIVERSITY OF HAWAII

THE LIFE CYCLE OF THE FLEA

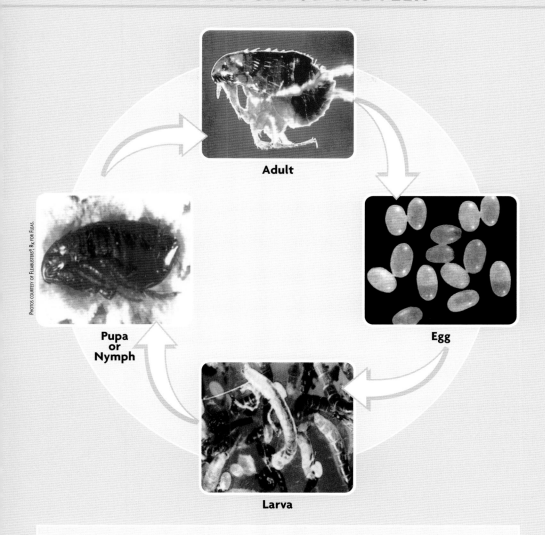

Adult

Egg

Larva

Pupa or Nymph

Fleas have been around for millions of years and have adapted to changing host animals. They are able to go through a complete life cycle in less than one month or they can extend their lives to almost two years by remaining as pupae or cocoons. They do not need blood or any other food for up to 20 months.

INSECT GROWTH REGULATOR

Two types of products should be used when treating fleas—a product to treat the pet and a product to treat the home. Adult fleas represent less than 1% of the flea population. The pre-adult fleas (eggs, larvae and pupae) represent more than 99% of the flea population and are found in the environment; it is in the case of pre-adult fleas that products containing an Insect Growth Regulator (IGR) should be used in the home.

IGRs are a new class of compounds used to prevent the development of insects. They do not kill the insect outright, but instead use the insect's biology against it to stop it from completing its growth. Products that contain methoprene are the world's first and leading IGRs. Used to control fleas and other insects, this type of IGR will stop flea larvae from developing and protect the house for up to seven months.

The American dog tick, *Dermacentor variabilis*, is probably the most common tick found on dogs. Look at the strength in its eight legs! No wonder it's hard to detach them.

The second stage of treatment is to apply an adult insecticide to the dog. Traditionally, this would be in the form of a collar or a spray, but more recent innovations include digestible insecticides that poison the fleas when they ingest the dog's blood. Alternatively, there are drops that, when placed on the back of the dog's neck, spread throughout the hair and skin to kill adult fleas.

TICKS

Though not as common as fleas, ticks are found all over the tropical and temperate world. They don't bite, like fleas; they harpoon. They dig their sharp proboscis (nose) into the dog's skin and drink the blood. Their

adult insecticides are only active for a few days.

When treating with a household spray, it is a good idea to vacuum before applying the product. This stimulates as many pupae as possible to hatch into adult fleas. The vacuum cleaner should also be treated with an insecticide to prevent the eggs and larvae that have been collected in the vacuum bag from hatching.

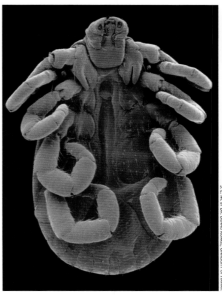

S. E. M. by Dr. Dennis Kunkel, University of Hawaii

only food and drink is dog's blood. Dogs can get Lyme disease, Rocky Mountain spotted fever, tick bite paralysis and many other diseases from ticks. They may live where fleas are found and they like to hide in cracks or seams in walls. They are controlled the same way fleas are controlled.

The American dog tick, *Dermacentor variabilis*, may well be the most common dog tick in many geographical areas, especially those areas where the climate is hot and humid. Most dog ticks have life expectancies of a week to six months, depending upon climatic conditions. They can neither jump nor fly, but they can crawl slowly and can range up to 16 feet to reach a sleeping or unsuspecting dog.

MITES

Just as fleas and ticks can be problematic for your dog, mites can also lead to an itchy nuisance. Microscopic in size, mites are related to ticks and generally take up permanent residence on their host animal—in this case, your dog! The term *mange* refers to any infestation caused by one of the mighty mites, of which there are six varieties that concern dog owners.

Demodex mites cause a condition known as demodicosis

DEER-TICK CROSSING

The great outdoors may be fun for your dog, but it also is a home to dangerous ticks. Deer ticks carry a bacterium known as *Borrelia burgdorferi* and are most active in the autumn and spring. When infections are caught early, penicillin and tetracycline are effective antibiotics, but, if left untreated, the bacteria may cause neurological, kidney and cardiac problems as well as long-term trouble with walking and painful joints.

S. E. M. BY DR. ANDREW SPIELMAN/PHOTOTAKE.

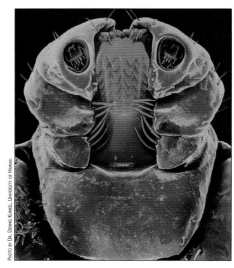

PHOTO BY DR. DENNIS KUNKEL, UNIVERSITY OF HAWAII.

The head of an American dog tick, *Dermacentor variabilis*, enlarged and colorized for effect.

133

**The mange mite,
Psoroptes bovis,
can infest cattle
and other
domestic animals.**

PHOTO BY JAMES HAYDEN/YOAV/PHOTOTAKE.

(sometimes called red mange or follicular mange), in which the mites live in the dog's hair follicles and sebaceous glands in larger-than-normal numbers. This type of mange is commonly passed from the dam to her puppies and usually shows up on the puppies' muzzles, though demodicosis is not transferable from one normal dog to another. Most dogs recover from this type of mange without any treatment, though topical therapies are commonly prescribed by the vet.

**Human lice look
like dog lice;
the two are
closely related.**

PHOTO BY DWIGHT R. KUHN.

The *Cheyletiellosis* mite is the hook-mouthed culprit associated with "walking dandruff," a condition that affects dogs as well as cats and rabbits. This mite lives on the surface of the animal's skin and is readily transferable through direct or indirect contact with an affected animal. The dandruff is present in the form of scaly skin, which may or may not be itchy. If not treated, this mange can affect a whole kennel of dogs and can be spread to humans as well.

The *Sarcoptes* mite causes intense itching on the dog in the form of a condition known as scabies or sarcoptic mange. The cycle of the *Sarcoptes* mite lasts about three weeks, and the mites live in the top layer of the dog's skin (epidermis), preferably in areas with little hair. Scabies is highly contagious and can be passed to humans. Sometimes an allergic reaction to the mite worsens the severe itching associated with sarcoptic mange.

Ear mites, *Otodectes cynotis,* lead to otodectic mange, which most commonly affects the outer ear canal of the dog, though other areas can be affected as well. Dogs with ear-mite infestation commonly scratch at their ears, causing further irritation, and shake their heads. Dark brown droppings in the outer ear confirm the diagnosis. Your vet can prescribe a treatment to flush out the ears and kill any eggs in the ears. A complete month of treatment is necessary to cure the mange.

Two other mites, less common in dogs, include *Dermanyssus gallinae* (the poultry or red mite) and *Eutrombicula alfreddugesi* (the North American mite associated with trombiculidiasis or chigger infestation). The poultry mite frequently lives on chickens, but can transfer to dogs who spend time near farm animals. Chigger infestation affects dogs in the

---

NOT A DROP TO DRINK

Never allow your dog to swim in polluted water or public areas where water quality can be suspect. Even perfectly clear water can harbor parasites, many of which can cause serious to fatal illnesses in canines. Areas inhabited by waterfowl and other wildlife are especially dangerous.

Central US who have exposure to woodlands. The types of mange caused by both of these mites are treatable by vets.

INTERNAL PARASITES

Most animals—fishes, birds and mammals, including dogs and humans—have worms and other parasites that live inside their bodies. According to Dr. Herbert R. Axelrod, the fish pathologist, there are two kinds of parasites: dumb and smart. The smart parasites live in peaceful cooperation with their hosts (symbiosis), while the dumb parasites kill their hosts. Most worm infections are relatively easy to control. If they are not controlled, they weaken the host dog to the point that other medical problems occur, but they do not kill the host as dumb parasites would.

A brown dog tick, *Rhipicephalus sanguineus*, is an uncommon but annoying tick found on dogs.
Photo by Carolina Biological Supply/Phototake.

DO NOT MIX

Never mix parasite-control products without first consulting your vet. Some products can become toxic when combined with others and can cause fatal consequences.

135

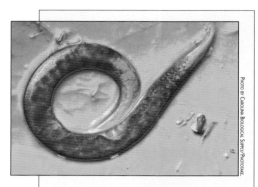

Photo by Carolina Biological Supply/Phototake

The roundworm *Rhabditis* can infect both dogs and humans.

ROUNDWORMS

Average-size dogs can pass 1,360,000 roundworm eggs every day. For example, if there were only 1 million dogs in the world, the world would be saturated with thousands of tons of dog feces. These feces would contain around 15,000,000,000 roundworm eggs.

Up to 31% of home yards and children's sand boxes in the US contain roundworm eggs.

Flushing dog's feces down the toilet is not a safe practice because the usual sewage treatments do not destroy roundworm eggs.

Infected puppies start shedding roundworm eggs at three weeks of age. They can be infected by their mother's milk.

The roundworm, *Ascaris lumbricoides.*

Photo by Dwight R. Kuhn.

ROUNDWORMS

The roundworms that infect dogs are known scientifically as *Toxocara canis*. They live in the dog's intestines and shed eggs continually. It has been estimated that a dog produces about 6 or more ounces of feces every day. Each ounce of feces averages hundreds of thousands of roundworm eggs. There are no known areas in which dogs roam that do not contain roundworm eggs. The greatest danger of roundworms is that they infect people, too! It is wise to have your dog tested regularly for roundworms.

In young puppies, roundworms cause bloated bellies, diarrhea, coughing and vomiting, and are transmitted from the dam (through blood or milk). Affected puppies will not appear as animated as normal puppies. The worms appear spaghetti-like, measuring as long as 6 inches. Adult dogs can acquire roundworms through coprophagia (eating contaminated feces) or by killing rodents that carry roundworms.

Roundworm infection can kill puppies and cause severe problems in adults, as the hatched larvae travel to the lungs and trachea through the bloodstream. Cleanliness is the best preventative for roundworms. Always pick up after your dog and dispose of feces in appropriate receptacles.

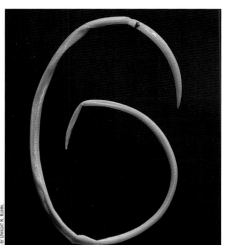

PHOTO BY DWIGHT R. KUHN.

HOOKWORMS

In the United States, dog owners have to be concerned about four different species of hookworm, the most common and most serious of which is *Ancylostoma caninum,* which prefers warm climates. The others are *Ancylostoma braziliense, Ancylostoma tubaeforme* and *Uncinaria stenocephala,* the latter of which is a concern to dogs living in the Northern US and Canada, as this species prefers cold climates. Hookworms are dangerous to humans as well as to dogs and cats, and can be the cause of severe anemia due to iron deficiency. The worm uses its teeth to attach itself to the dog's intestines and changes the site of its attachment about six times per day. Each time the worm repositions itself, the dog loses blood and can become anemic. *Ancylostoma caninum* is the most likely of the four species to cause anemia in the dog.

Symptoms of hookworm infection include dark stools, weight loss, general weakness, pale coloration and anemia, as well as possible skin problems. Fortunately, hookworms are easily purged from the affected dog with a number of medications that have proven effective. Discuss these with your vet. Most heartworm preventatives include a hookworm insecticide as well.

Owners also must be aware that hookworms can infect humans, who can acquire the larvae through exposure to contaminated feces. Since the worms cannot complete their life cycle on a human, the worms simply infest the skin and cause irritation. This condition is known as cutaneous larva migrans syndrome. As a preventative, use disposable gloves or a "poop-scoop" to pick up your dog's droppings and prevent your dog (or neighborhood cats) from defecating in children's play areas.

The hookworm, *Ancylostoma caninum*.

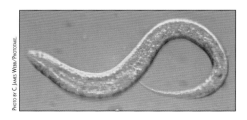

PHOTO BY C. JAMES WEBB/ PHOTOTAKE.

The infective stage of the hookworm larva.

137

TAPEWORMS

Humans, rats, squirrels, foxes, coyotes, wolves and domestic dogs are all susceptible to tapeworm infection. Except in humans, tapeworms are usually not a fatal infection. Infected individuals can harbor 1000 parasitic worms.

Tapeworms, like some other types of worm, are hermaphroditic, meaning male and female in the same worm.

If dogs eat infected rats or mice, or anything else infected with tapeworm, they get the tapeworm disease. One month after attaching to a dog's intestine, the worm starts shedding eggs. These eggs are infective immediately. Infective eggs can live for a few months without a host animal.

The head and rostellum (the round prominence on the scolex) of a tapeworm, which infects dogs and humans.

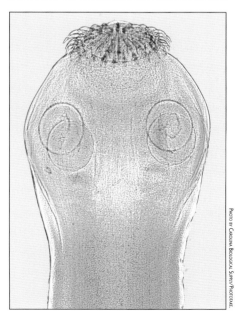

PHOTO BY CAROLINA BIOLOGICAL SUPPLY/PHOTOTAKE.

TAPEWORMS

There are many species of tapeworm, all of which are carried by fleas! The most common tapeworm affecting dogs is known as *Dipylidium caninum*. The dog eats the flea and starts the tapeworm cycle. Humans can also be infected with tapeworms—so don't eat fleas! Fleas are so small that your dog could pass them onto your hands, your plate or your food and thus make it possible for you to ingest a flea that is carrying tapeworm eggs.

While tapeworm infection is not life-threatening in dogs (smart parasite!), it can be the cause of a very serious liver disease for humans. About 50% of the humans infected with *Echinococcus multilocularis*, a type of tapeworm that causes alveolar hydatid, perish.

WHIPWORMS

In North America, whipworms are counted among the most common parasitic worms in dogs. The whipworm's scientific name is *Trichuris vulpis*. These worms attach themselves in the lower parts of the intestine, where they feed. Affected dogs may only experience upset tummies, colic and diarrhea. These worms, however, can live for months or years in the dog, beginning their larval stage in the small intestine, spending their adult stage in the large intestine and finally passing infective eggs through the dog's feces. The only way to detect whipworms is through a fecal examination, though this is not always foolproof. Treatment for whipworms is tricky, due to the worms' unusual life-cycle pattern, and very often dogs are reinfected due to exposure to infective eggs on the ground. The whipworm eggs can survive in the environment for as long as five years; thus, cleaning up droppings in your own backyard as well as in public places is absolutely essential for sanitation purposes and the health of your dog and others.

THREADWORMS

Though less common than roundworms, hookworms and those previously mentioned, threadworms concern dog owners in the Southwestern US and Gulf Coast area where the climate is hot and humid. Living in the small intestine of the dog, this worm measures a mere 2 millimeters and is round in shape. Like that of the whipworm, the threadworm's life cycle is very complex and the eggs and larvae are passed through the feces. A deadly disease in humans, *Strongyloides* readily infects people, and the handling of feces is the most common means of transmission. Threadworms are most often seen in young puppies; bloody diarrhea and pneumonia are symptoms. Sick puppies must be isolated and treated immediately; vets recommend a follow-up treatment one month later.

HEARTWORM PREVENTATIVES

There are many heartworm preventatives on the market, many of which are sold at your veterinarian's office. These products can be given daily or monthly, depending on the manufacturer's instructions. All of these preventatives contain chemical insecticides directed at killing heartworms, which leads to some controversy among dog owners. In effect, heartworm preventatives are necessary evils, though you should determine how necessary based on your pet's lifestyle. There is no doubt that heartworm is a dreadful disease that threatens the lives of dogs. However, the likelihood of your dog's being bitten by an infected mosquito is slim in most places, and a mosquito-repellent (or an herbal remedy such as Wormwood or Black Walnut) is much safer for your dog and will not compromise his immune system (the way heartworm preventatives will). Should you decide to use the traditional preventative "medications," you can consider giving the pill every other or third month. Since the toxins in the pill will kill the heartworms at all stages of development, the pill would be effective in killing larvae, nymphs or adults, and it takes four months for the larvae to reach the adult stage. Thus, there is no rationale to poisoning the dog's system on a monthly basis. Lastly, do not give the pill during the winter months, since there are no mosquitoes around to pass on their infection, unless you live in a tropical environment.

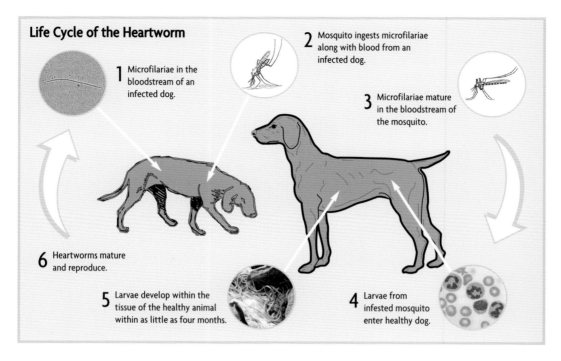

Life Cycle of the Heartworm

1 Microfilariae in the bloodstream of an infected dog.

2 Mosquito ingests microfilariae along with blood from an infected dog.

3 Microfilariae mature in the bloodstream of the mosquito.

6 Heartworms mature and reproduce.

5 Larvae develop within the tissue of the healthy animal within as little as four months.

4 Larvae from infested mosquito enter healthy dog.

HEARTWORMS

Heartworms are thin, extended worms up to 12 inches long, which live in a dog's heart and the major blood vessels surrounding it. Dogs may have up to 200 worms. Symptoms may be loss of energy, loss of appetite, coughing, the development of a pot belly and anemia.

Heartworms are transmitted by mosquitoes. The mosquito drinks the blood of an infected dog and takes in larvae with the blood. The larvae, called microfilariae, develop within the body of the mosquito and are passed on to the next dog bitten after the larvae mature. It takes two to three weeks for the larvae to develop to the infective stage within the body of the mosquito. Dogs are usually treated at about six weeks of age and maintained on a prophylactic dose given monthly.

Blood testing for heartworms is not necessarily indicative of how seriously your dog is infected. Although this is a dangerous disease, it is not easy for a dog to be infected. Discuss the various preventatives with your vet, as there are many different types now available. Together you can decide on a safe course of prevention for your dog.

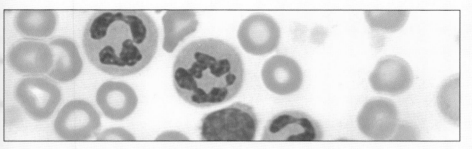

Magnified heartworm larvae, *Dirofilaria immitis.*

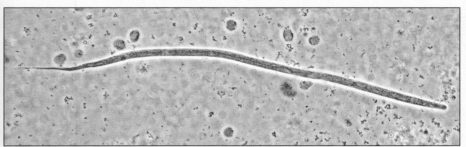

Heartworm, *Dirofilaria immitis.*

The heart of a dog infected with canine heartworm, *Dirofilaria immitis.*

HOMEOPATHY:
an alternative to medicine

"Less is Most"

Using this principle, the strength of a homeopathic remedy is measured by the number of serial dilutions that were undertaken to create it. The greater the number of serial dilutions, the greater the strength of the homeopathic remedy. The potency of a remedy that has been made by making a dilution of 1 part in 100 parts (or 1/100) is 1c or 1cH. If this remedy is subjected to a series of further dilutions, each one being 1/100, a more dilute and stronger remedy is produced. If the remedy is diluted in this way six times, it is called 6c or 6cH. A dilution of 6c is 1 part in 1000,000,000,000. In general, higher potencies in more frequent doses are better for acute symptoms and lower potencies in more infrequent doses are more useful for chronic, long-standing problems.

CURING OUR DOGS NATURALLY

Holistic medicine means treating the whole animal as a unique, perfect living being. Generally, holistic treatments do not suppress the symptoms that the body naturally produces, as do most medications prescribed by conventional doctors and vets. Holistic methods seek to cure disease by regaining balance and harmony in the patient's environment. Some of these methods include use of nutritional therapy, herbs, flower essences, aromatherapy, acupuncture, massage, chiropractic and, of course the most popular holistic approach, homeopathy.

Homeopathy is a theory or system of treating illness with small doses of substances which, if administered in larger quantities, would produce the symptoms that the patient already has. This approach is often described as "like cures like." Although modern veterinary medicine is geared toward the "quick fix," homeopathy relies on the belief that, given the time, the body is able to heal itself and return to its natural, healthy state.

Choosing a remedy to cure a problem in our dogs is the difficult part of homeopathy. Consult with your veterinarian for a professional diagnosis of your dog's symptoms. Often these symptoms require immediate conventional care. If your vet is willing, and knowledgeable, you may attempt a homeopathic remedy. Be aware that cortisone prevents homeopathic remedies from working. There are hundreds of possibilities and combinations to cure many problems in dogs, from basic physical problems such as excessive shedding, fleas or other parasites, unattractive doggy odor, bad breath, upset stomach, obesity, dry, oily or dull coat, diarrhea, ear problems or eye discharge (including tears and dry or mucusy matter), to behavioral abnormalities, such as fear of loud noises, habitual licking, poor appetite, excessive barking and various phobias. From alumina to zincum metallicum, the remedies span the planet and the imagination...from flowers and weeds to chemicals, insect droppings, diesel smoke and volcanic ash.

Using "Like to Treat Like"

Unlike conventional medicines that suppress symptoms, homeopathic remedies treat illnesses with small doses of substances that, if administered in larger quantities, would produce the symptoms that the patient already has. While the same homeopathic remedy can be used to treat different symptoms in different dogs, here are some interesting remedies and their uses.

Apis Mellifica
(made from honey bee venom) can be used for allergies or to reduce swelling that occurs in acutely infected kidneys.

Diesel Smoke
can be used to help control motion sickness.

Calcarea Fluorica
(made from calcium fluoride, which helps harden bone structure) can be useful in treating hard lumps in tissues.

Natrum Muriaticum
(made from common salt, sodium chloride) is useful in treating thin, thirsty dogs.

Nitricum Acidum
(made from nitric acid) is used for symptoms you would expect to see from contact with acids such as lesions, especially where the skin joins the linings of body orifices or openings such as the lips and nostrils.

Symphytum
(made from the herb Knitbone, *Symphytum officinale*) is used to encourage bones to heal.

Urtica Urens
(made from the common stinging nettle) is used in treating painful, irritating rashes.

143

HOMEOPATHIC REMEDIES FOR YOUR DOG

Symptom/Ailment	Possible Remedy
ALLERGIES	Apis Mellifica 30c, Astacus Fluviatilis 6c, Pulsatilla 30c, Urtica Urens 6c
ALOPECIA	Alumina 30c, Lycopodium 30c, Sepia 30c, Thallium 6c
ANAL GLANDS (BLOCKED)	Hepar Sulphuris Calcareum 30c, Sanicula 6c, Silicea 6c
ARTHRITIS	Rhus Toxicodendron 6c, Bryonia Alba 6c
CANINE COUGH	Drosera 6c, Ipecacuanha 30c
CATARACT	Calcarea Carbonica 6c, Conium Maculatum 6c, Phosphorus 30c, Silicea 30c
CONSTIPATION	Alumina 6c, Carbo Vegetabilis 30c, Graphites 6c, Nitricum Acidum 30c, Silicea 6c
COUGHING	Aconitum Napellus 6c, Belladonna 30c, Hyoscyamus Niger 30c, Phosphorus 30c
DIARRHEA	Arsenicum Album 30c, Aconitum Napellus 6c, Chamomilla 30c, Mercurius Corrosivus 30c
DRY EYE	Zincum Metallicum 30c
EAR PROBLEMS	Aconitum Napellus 30c, Belladonna 30c, Hepar Sulphuris 30c, Tellurium 30c, Psorinum 200c
EYE PROBLEMS	Borax 6c, Aconitum Napellus 30c, Graphites 6c, Staphysagria 6c, Thuja Occidentalis 30c
GLAUCOMA	Aconitum Napellus 30c, Apis Mellifica 6c, Phosphorus 30c
HEAT STROKE	Belladonna 30c, Gelsemium Sempervirens 30c, Sulphur 30c
HICCUPS	Cinchona Deficinalis 6c
HIP DYSPLASIA	Colocynthis 6c, Rhus Toxicodendron 6c, Bryonia Alba 6c
INCONTINENCE	Argentum Nitricum 6c, Causticum 30c, Conium Maculatum 30c, Pulsatilla 30c, Sepia 30c
INSECT BITES	Apis Mellifica 30c, Cantharis 30c, Hypericum Perforatum 6c, Urtica Urens 30c
ITCHING	Alumina 30c, Arsenicum Album 30c, Carbo Vegetabilis 30c, Hypericum Perforatum 6c, Mezerium 6c, Sulphur 30c
MASTITIS	Apis Mellifica 30c, Belladonna 30c, Urtica Urens 1m
MOTION SICKNESS	Cocculus 6c, Petroleum 6c
PATELLAR LUXATION	Gelsemium Sempervirens 6c, Rhus Toxicodendron 6c
PENIS PROBLEMS	Aconitum Napellus 30c, Hepar Sulphuris Calcareum 30c, Pulsatilla 30c, Thuja Occidentalis 6c
PUPPY TEETHING	Calcarea Carbonica 6c, Chamomilla 6c, Phytolacca 6c

Recognizing a Sick Dog

Unlike colicky babies and cranky children, our canine kids cannot tell us when they are feeling ill. Therefore, there are a number of signs that owners can identify to know that their dogs are not feeling well.

**Take note for
physical manifestations such as:**

- unusual, bad odor, including bad breath
- excessive shedding
- wax in the ears, chronic ear irritation
- oily, flaky, dull haircoat
- mucus, tearing or similar discharge in the eyes
- fleas or mites
- mucus in stool, diarrhea
- sensitivity to petting or handling
- licking at paws, scratching face, etc.

**Keep an eye out for
behavioral changes as well including:**

- lethargy, idleness
- lack of patience or general irritability
- lack of interest in food
- phobias (fear of people, loud noises, etc.)
- strange behavior, suspicion, fear
- coprophagia
- more frequent barking
- whimpering, crying

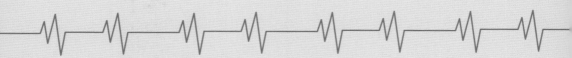

Get Well Soon

You don't need a DVM to provide good TLC to your sick or recovering dog, but you do need to pay attention to some details that normally wouldn't bother him. The following tips will aid Fido's recovery and get him back on his paws again:

- Keep his space free of irritating smells, like heavy perfumes and air fresheners.
- Rest is the best medicine! Avoid harsh lighting that will prevent your dog from sleeping. Shade him from bright sunlight during the day and dim the lights in the evening.
- Keep the noise level down. Animals are more sensitive to sound when they are sick.

- Be attentive to any necessary temperature adjustments. A dog with a fever needs a cool room and cold liquids. A bitch that is whelping or recovering from surgery will be more comfortable in a warm room, consuming warm liquids and food.
- You wouldn't send a sick child back to school early, so don't rush your dog back into a full routine until he seems absolutely ready.

Neatness Counts

Surely you've spent hours grooming your dog to perfection for the show ring, but don't forget about yourself! While the dog should be the center of attention, it is important that you also appear neat and clean. Wear

smart, appropriate clothes and comfortable shoes in a color that contrasts with your dog's coat. Look and act like a professional.

When you purchase your Dachshund, you will make it clear to the breeder whether you want one just as a loveable companion and pet, or if you hope to be buying a Dachshund with show prospects. No reputable breeder will sell you a young puppy and tell you that it is *definitely* of show quality, for so much can go wrong during the early months of a puppy's development. If you plan to show, what you will hopefully have acquired is a puppy with "show potential."

To the novice, exhibiting a Dachshund in the show ring may look easy, but it takes a lot of hard work and devotion to do top winning at a show such as the prestigious Westminster Kennel Club dog show, not to mention a little luck too!

The first concept that the canine novice learns when watching a dog show is that each dog first competes against members of its own breed. Once the judge has selected the best member of each breed (Best of Breed), that chosen dog will compete with other dogs in its group. Finally, the dogs chosen first in each group will compete for Best in Show.

The second concept that you must understand is that the dogs are not actually compared against one another. The judge compares each dog against its breed standard, the written description of the ideal specimen that is approved by the American Kennel Club (AKC). While some early breed standards were indeed based on specific dogs that were famous or popular, many dedicated enthusiasts say that a perfect specimen, as described in the standard, has never walked into a show ring, has never been bred and, to the woe of dog breeders around the globe, does not exist. Breeders attempt to get as close to this ideal as possible with every litter, but theoretically the "perfect" dog is so elusive that it is impossible. (And if the "perfect" dog were born, breeders and judges probably would never agree that it was indeed "perfect.")

If you are interested in exploring the world of dog showing, your best bet is to join your local breed club or the national (or parent) club, which is the Dachshund Club of America. These clubs often host both regional and national specialties, shows only for Dachshunds, which can include conformation as well as obedience and field trials. Even if you have no intention of competing with your Dachshund, a specialty is like a

PRACTICE AT HOME

If you have decided to show your dog, you must train him to gait around the ring by your side at the correct pace and pattern, and to tolerate being handled and examined by the judge. Most breeds

require complete dentition, all breeds require a particular bite (scissors, level or undershot) and all males must have two apparently normal testicles fully descended into the scrotum. Enlist family and friends to hold mock trials in your yard to prepare your future champion!

festival for lovers of the breed who congregate to share their favorite topic: Dachshunds! Clubs also send out newsletters, and some organize training days and seminars in order that people may learn more about their chosen breed. To locate the breed club closest to you, contact the American Kennel Club, which furnishes the rules and regulations for all of these events plus general dog registration and other basic requirements of dog ownership.

TEMPERAMENT PLUS

Although it seems that physical conformation is the only factor considered in the show ring, temperament is also of utmost importance. An aggressive or fearful dog should not be shown. Bad behavior will not be tolerated and may pose a threat to the judge, other exhibitors, you and your dog, and usually results in disqualification.

In the US, the American Kennel Club offers three kinds of conformation shows: an all-breed show (for all AKC-recognized breeds), a specialty show (for one breed only, usually sponsored by the parent club) and a group show (for all breeds in the group).

For a dog to become an AKC champion of record, the dog must accumulate 15 points at shows from at least three different judges, including two "majors." A "major" is defined as a three-, four- or five-point win, and the number of points per win is determined on the number of dogs entered in the show on that day. Depending on the breed, the number of points that are awarded varies. In a breed as popular as the Dachshund, more dogs are needed to rack up the points. At any dog show, only one dog and one bitch of each breed can win points.

Dog showing does not offer "co-ed" classes. Dogs and bitches never compete against each other in the classes. Non-champions are called "class dogs" because they compete in one of five classes. Dogs are entered in particular classes depending on their age and previous show wins. To begin, there is the Puppy Class (for 6- to 9-month-olds and for 9- to 12-month-olds); this class is followed by the Novice Class (for dogs that have not won any first prizes except in the Puppy Class or three first prizes in the Novice Class and have not accumulated any points toward their champion title); the Bred-by-Exhibitor Class (for dogs handled by their breeders or handled by one of the breeder's immediate family); the American-bred Class (for dogs bred in the USA!); and the Open Class (for any dog that is not a champion).

The judge at the show begins by judging the Puppy Class, first dogs and then bitches, and proceeds through the classes. The judge places his winners first through fourth in each class. In the Winners Class, the first-place winners of each class compete with one another to determine Winners Dog and Winners Bitch. The judge also places a Reserve Winners Dog and Reserve Winners Bitch, which could be awarded the points in the case of a disqualification. The Winners Dog and Winners Bitch are the two that are awarded the points for the breed, then compete with any champions of record entered in the show. The judge reviews the Winners Dog, Winners Bitch and all of the champions to select his Best of Breed. The Best of Winners is selected between the Winners Dog and Winners Bitch. Were one of these two to be selected Best of Breed, it would automatically be named Best of Winners as well. Finally the judge selects his Best of Opposite Sex to the Best of Breed winner.

At a group show or all-breed show, the Best of Breed winners from each breed then compete against one another in their respective groups for Group One through Group Four. The judge compares each Best of Breed to its breed standard, and the dog that most closely lives up to the ideal for its breed is selected as Group One. Finally, all seven group winners (from the Hound Group, Sporting Group, Toy Group, etc.) compete for Best in Show.

To find out about dog shows in your area, you can subscribe to the American Kennel Club's monthly magazine, the *American Kennel Gazette* and the accompanying Events Calendar. You can also look in your local newspaper for advertisements for dog shows in your area or go on the Internet to the AKC's website, http:www.akc.org.

Physical Exam

Dachshunds, like other small breeds and the Toy breeds, are put on a table in the show ring to be evaluated by the judge. This raises the dog to the judge's height, allowing

the judge to get a close overall look at the dog and perform a careful "hands-on" examination of the dog's structure. These procedures are the telling signs of how well each dog's physical conformation matches that of the ideal set forth in the breed standard, the measuring stick against which all show dogs are considered.

If your Dachshund is six months of age or older and registered with the AKC, you can enter him in a dog show where the breed is offered classes. Provided that your Dachshund does not have a disqualifying fault, he can compete. Only unaltered dogs can be entered in a dog show, so if you have spayed or neutered your Dachshund, he cannot compete in conformation shows. The reason for this is simple. Dog shows are the main forum to prove which representatives in a breed are worthy of being bred. Only dogs that have achieved championships—the AKC "seal of approval" for quality in pure-bred dogs—- should be bred. Altered dogs, however, can participate in other AKC events such as obedience trials and the Canine Good Citizen program.

Before you actually step into the ring, you would be well advised to sit back and observe the judge's ring procedure. If it is your first time in the ring, do not be over-anxious and run to the front of the line. It is much better to stand back and study how the exhibitor in front of you is performing. The judge asks each handler to stand, or "stack," the dog, hopefully showing the dog off to his best advantage. The judge will observe the dog from a distance and from different angles, and approach the dog to check his teeth, overall structure, alertness and muscle tone, as well as consider how well the dog "conforms" to the standard. Most importantly, the judge will have the exhibitor move the dog

around the ring in some pattern that he should specify (another advantage to not going first, but always listen since some judges change their directions—and the judge is always right!). Finally, the judge will give the dog one last look before moving on to the next exhibitor.

If you are not in the top four in your class at your first show, do not be discouraged. Be patient and consistent, and you may eventually find yourself in a winning line-up. Remember that the winners were once in your shoes and have devoted many hours and much money to earn the placement. If you find that your dog is losing every time and never getting a nod, it may be time to consider a different dog sport or to just enjoy your Dachshund as a pet. Parent clubs offer other events, such as agility, tracking, obedience, instinct tests and more, which may be of interest to the owner of a well-trained Dachshund.

EARTHDOG TESTS
Interest in promoting the natural ability of Dachshunds has exploded in the US, and earthdog tests, sponsored by the American Kennel Club, have become an exciting part of Dachshund ownership. These tests are enjoyed by the show-dog set as well as by everyday pet owners. The only Hound in the group

bred to go to ground after quarry, the Dachshund is happy to be the guest of the traditional Terrier breeds, for whom the tests are largely geared. According to AKC rules, Dachshunds must be six months of age to participate in the tests and can compete at four class levels, including Introduction to Quarry, Junior Earthdog, Senior Earthdog and Master Earthdog. Artificial or live quarry is used in these tests, though cages protect the rats from physical (if not psychological) harm. The stated purpose of earthdog tests is to provide the dogs the chance to demonstrate their natural talent in following and pursuing game.

FIELD TRIALS

Field trials are offered to the retrievers, pointers and spaniel breeds of the Sporting Group as well as to the Beagles, Dachshunds and Bassets of the Hound Group. The purpose of field trials is to demonstrate a dog's ability to perform its original purpose in the field. The events vary depending on the type of dog, but in all trials dogs compete against one another for placement and for points toward their Field Champion (FC) titles.

Dachshunds participate in trials similar to those used for Beagles and Basset Hounds. The main purpose of the trial is to trail a rabbit, whether in a brace

BECOMING A CHAMPION

An official AKC champion of record requires that a dog accumulate 15 points under three different judges, including two "majors" under different judges. Points are awarded based on the number of dogs entered into competition,

varying from breed to breed and place to place. A win of three, four or five points is considered a "major." The AKC assigns a schedule of points annually to adjust to the variations that accompany a breed's popularity and the population of a given area.

(a pair) or in small groups. The trial is judged based on the Dachshund's accuracy in following its quarry.

TRACKING

Any dog is capable of tracking, using its nose to follow a trail. The Dachshund's superb scenting

Dachshund

Inquire about earthdog events in your part of the country. The American Kennel Club or the Dachshund Club of America can provide you with more information about these trials.

ability and low-to-the-ground stature make him ideally suited for tracking tests. The AKC started tracking tests in 1937, when the first licensed test took place as part of the Utility level at an obedience trial. Ten years later, in 1947, the AKC offered the first title, Tracking Dog (TD). It was not until 1980 that the AKC added the Tracking Dog Excellent title (TDX), which was followed by the Versatile Surface Tracking title (VST) in 1995. The title Champion Tracker (CT) is awarded to a dog who has earned all three titles.

OBEDIENCE TRIALS

Obedience trials in the US trace back to the early 1930s, when organized obedience training was developed to demonstrate how well dog and owner could work together. The pioneer of obedience trials is Mrs. Helen Whitehouse Walker, a Standard Poodle fancier, who designed a series of exercises after the Associated Sheep, Police Army Dog Society of Great Britain. Since the days of Mrs. Walker, obedience trials have grown by leaps and bounds, and today there are over 2,000 trials held in the US every year, with more than 100,000 dogs competing. Any registered AKC or ILP (Indefinite Listing Privilege) dog can enter an obedience trial, regardless of conformational disqualifications or neutering.

Obedience trials are divided into three levels of progressive difficulty. At the first level, the Novice, dogs compete for the title Companion Dog (CD); at the intermediate level, the Open, dogs compete for the title Companion Dog Excellent (CDX); and at the advanced level, dogs compete for the title Utility Dog (UD). Classes are sub-divided into "A" (for beginners) and "B" (for more experienced handlers). A perfect score at any level is 200, and a dog must score 170 or better to earn a "leg," of which three are needed to earn the title.

To earn points, the dog must score more than 50% of the available points in each exercise; the possible points range from 20 to 40.

Once a dog has earned the UD title, he can compete with other proven obedience dogs for the coveted title of Utility Dog Excellent (UDX), which requires that the dog win "legs" in ten shows. In 1977, the title Obedience Trial Champion (OTCh.) was established by the AKC. Utility Dogs who earn "legs" in Open B and Utility B earn points toward their Obedience Trial Champion title. To become an OTCh., a dog needs to earn 100 points, which requires three first places in Open B and Utility under three different judges.

The Grand Prix of obedience trials, the AKC National Obedience Invitational, gives qualifying Utility Dogs the chance to win the newest and highest title: National Obedience Champion (NOC). Only the top 25 ranked obedience dogs, plus any dog ranked in the top 3 in its breed, are allowed to compete.

AGILITY TRIALS
Having had its origins in the UK back in 1977, AKC agility had its official beginning in the US in

When properly trained, a Dachshund can be trained for working and agility trials. When observers see this little bundle of energy going through the trials, they applaud enthusiastically at seeing the agile and animated Dachshund.

KENNEL CLUBS

You can get information about dog shows from the national kennel clubs:

American Kennel Club
5580 Centerview Dr., Raleigh, NC 27606-3390
www.akc.org

United Kennel Club
100 E. Kilgore Road, Kalamazoo, MI 49002
www.ukcdogs.com

Canadian Kennel Club
89 Skyway Ave., Suite 100, Etobicoke, Ontario M9W 6R4 Canada
www.ckc.ca

The Kennel Club
1-5 Clarges St., Piccadilly,
London W1Y 8AB, UK
www.the-kennel-club.org.uk

August 1994, when the first licensed agility trials were held. The AKC allows all registered breeds (including Miscellaneous Class breeds) to participate, providing the dog is 12 months of age or older. Agility is designed so that the handler demonstrates how well the dog can work at his side. The handler directs his dog over an obstacle course that includes jumps as well as tires, the dog walk, weave poles, pipe tunnels, collapsed tunnels, etc. While working his way through the course, the dog must keep one eye and ear on the handler and the rest of his body on the course. The handler gives verbal and hand signals to guide the dog through the course.

The first organization to promote agility trials in the US was the United States Dog Agility Association, Inc. (USDAA), which was established in 1986 and spawned numerous member clubs around the country. Both the USDAA and the AKC offer titles to winning dogs. Three titles are available through the USDAA: Agility Dog (AD), Advanced Agility Dog (AAD) and Master Agility Dog (MAD). The AKC offers Novice Agility (NA), Open Agility (OA), Agility Excellent (AX) and Master Agility Excellent (MX). Beyond these four AKC titles, dogs can win additional ones in "jumper" classes, Jumpers with Weave Novice (NAJ), Open (OAJ) and Excellent (MXJ), which lead to the ultimate title(s): MACH, Master Agility Champion. Dogs can continue to add number designations to the MACH titles, indicating how many times the dog has met the MACH require-ments, such as MACH1, MACH2, etc.

Agility is great fun for dog and owner, with many rewards for everyone involved. Interested owners should join a training club that has obstacles and experienced agility handlers who can introduce you and your dog to the "ropes" (and tires, tunnels, etc.).

AMERICAN KENNEL CLUB TITLES

The AKC offers over 40 different titles to dogs in competition. Depending on the events that your dog can enter, different titles apply. Some titles can be applied as prefixes, meaning that they are placed before the dog's name (e.g., Ch. King of the Road) and others are used as suffixes, placed after the dog's name (e.g., King of the Road, CD).

These titles are used as prefixes:

Conformation Dog Shows
- Ch. (Champion)

Obedience Trials
- NOC (National Obedience Champion)
- OTCH (Obedience Trial Champion)
- VCCH (Versatile Companion Champion)

Tracking Tests
- CT [Champion Tracker (TD,TDX and VST)]

Agility Trials
- MACH (Master Agility Champion)
- MACH2, MACH3, MACH4, etc.

Field Trials
- FC (Field Champion)
- AFC (Amateur Field Champion)
- NFC (National Field Champion)
- NAFC (National Amateur Field Champion)
- NOGDC (National Open Gun Dog Champion)
- AKC GDSC (AKC Gun Dog Stake Champion)
- AKC RGDSC (AKC Retrieving Gun Dog Stake Champion)

Herding Trials
- HC (Herding Champion)

Dual
- DC (Dual Champion — Ch. and FC)

Triple
- TC (Triple Champion — Ch., FC and OTCH)

Coonhounds
- NCH (Nite Champion)
- GNCH (Grand Nite Champion)
- SHNCH (Senior Grand Nite Champion)
- GCH (Senior Champion)
- SGCH (Senior Grand Champion)
- GFC (Grand Field Champion)
- SGFC (Senior Grand Field Champion)
- WCH (Water Race Champion)
- GWCH (Water Race Grand Champion)
- SGWCH (Senior Grand Water Race Champion)

These titles are used as suffixes:

Obedience
- CD (Companion Dog)
- CDX (Companion Dog Excellent)
- UD (Utility Dog)
- UDX (Utility Dog Excellent)
- VCD1 (Versatile Companion Dog 1)
- VCD2 (Versatile Companion Dog 2)
- VCD3 (Versatile Companion Dog 3)
- VCD4 (Versatile Companion Dog 4)

Tracking Tests
- TD (Tracking Dog)
- TDX (Tracking Dog Excellent)
- VST (Variable Surface Tracker)

Agility Trials
- NA (Novice Agility)
- OA (Open Agility)
- AX (Agility Excellent)
- MX (Master Agility Excellent)
- NAJ (Novice Jumpers with weaves)
- OAJ (Open Jumpers with weaves)
- AXJ (Excellent Jumpers with weaves)
- MXJ (Master Excellent Jumpers with weaves)

Hunting Test
- JH (Junior Hunter)
- SH (Senior Hunter)
- MH (Master Hunter)

Herding Test
- HT (Herding Tested)
- PT (Pre-Trial Tested)
- HS (Herding Started)
- HI (Herding Intermediate)
- HX (Herding Excellent)

Lure Coursing
- JC (Junior Courser)
- SC (Senior Courser)
- MC (Master Courser)

Earthdog
- JE (Junior Earthdog)
- SE (Senior Earthdog)
- ME (Master Earthdog)

Lure Coursing
- JC (Junior Courser)
- SC (Senior Courser)
- MC (Master Courser)

INDEX

My Dachshund

PUT YOUR PUPPY'S FIRST PICTURE HERE

Dog's Name _____

Date _____ Photographer _____